Ian Vince was born in Brig[...] an administrative nightma[...] around the country, going t[...] the doctor, the dentist, sig......g on, paying tax and, finally, writing books, one of which you are holding now. Before he wrote this book, he wrote and designed two others: *Britain: What A State* in 2005 and, with Dan Kieran, *The Myway Code* in 2006. Ian also writes for TV and print: he has a regular column in the *Daily Telegraph* and is a contributing editor of the magazine of easy living, the *Idler*. He lives in Salisbury with his wife, young daughter and a large unused filing cabinet.

The
Little Black Book
of Red Tape

TALES OF RED TAPE
AND JOBSWORTHS

Ian Vince

An Orion paperback

First published in Great Britain in 2007
by Orion
This paperback edition published in 2008
by Orion Books Ltd,
Orion House, 5 Upper St Martin's Lane,
London WC2H 9EA

An Hachette Livre UK company

1 3 5 7 9 10 8 6 4 2

A CIP catalogue record for this book is available
from the British Library.

ISBN 978-0-7528-9379-2

Printed and bound in Great Britain by Clays Ltd, St Ives plc

The Orion Publishing Group's policy is to use papers that
are natural, renewable and recyclable products and
made from wood grown in sustainable forests. The logging
and manufacturing processes are expected to conform to
the environmental regulations of the country of origin.

www.orionbooks.co.uk

To our beautiful daughter Freya,
who made all of this seem so simple.

CONTENTS

INTRODUCTION

To get the attention of a large animal, be it an elephant or a bureaucracy, it helps to know what part of it feels pain. Be very sure, though, that you want its full attention.
Kelvin Throop

This book is all about people's experiences with the official world. When I say 'official', I am referring not only to the whole beige panoply of councils, departments and ministries of state; but also to petty bureaucrats, jobsworths and a motley selection of twittering imbeciles from many kinds of different organisations. From car parking contractors to online auction sites, from public to private organisations, they all have their own counter-intuitive rules, regulations and 'red tape' to inflict on the rest of us.

In the following chapters you will find a number of encounters between this official world and ordinary members of the public, with the occasional internal bout between warring departments thrown in for good measure. No matter who's pitted against who, almost all of the anecdotes have a common thread – the trouble truly starts when the procedure not only gets in the way of the result, it actually becomes more important.

Almost everyone has a story about a difficult form, a nonsensical government department, an unhelpful call centre or an encounter with a power-hungry jobsworth intent on ruining their day.

For example, you may have been patiently making your way up a telephone queuing system, only to have your call dropped unceremoniously after 35 minutes. That is 35 minutes of low-fidelity tape loop, über-perky announcements and bland reassurances – against all the evidence provided – of the importance of your call. But it's also over half an hour you can never reclaim, 35 minutes of frustration and niggling discontent that there is no operator ready to take your call, that there is probably no representative busy with another customer. Perhaps there is nobody in the call centre at all – an abandoned floor of an empty building recharged with melancholy and resentment each day by a thousand people alternately sighing and belching obscenities from afar into their telephone handsets.

Or maybe you have been required to fill in a dozen pages of invasive paperwork, only to be told that it was 'the wrong form'. Sensing your difficulty with this pointless monomania, staff then treat you like a buffoon and issue you leaflets on how to fill in further leaflets.

The stories in this book highlight particular cases where twisted lines of communications and the odd obstructive member of front-line staff have conspired to make something that should be simple, very complicated indeed. But the bureaucratic system, with its undue emphasis on procedure and rules encourages silliness all the way up the chain of command.

As a ready example, who thought that it was acceptable to produce official paperwork for the attention of the recently bereaved that is so complex and twisted that one, four-page form has 24 pages of separate explanatory notes which, in turn, are accompanied by 14 pages of extra notes that provide further explanation of the explanatory notes? Why was the unit which presided over this mean-spirited enterprise simply not taken outside and shot through the lungs with high-velocity HB pencils?

Who decided that it was a great idea to play their disgruntled customers *Eine Kleine Nachtmusik* arranged for the accordion and spoons as hold muzak, and should they, indeed, be nailed to the back of a heavy door with croquet hoops as soon as a suitable supplier is found?

While compiling this collection of stories, I received a particularly concerned email from what would seem to be a particularly concerned civil servant.

'I am a civil servant (not the kind depicted in *Spooks* or the Whitehall variety),' begins the email, with a flourish of irrelevance. 'All I have to say is that the vast majority of civil servants are just that… public servants, and happy to be that. What really screws everything up is the bone-headed intervention of management; the kind of corporate wankers and politicians who by some miracle of evolution have been deigned to be worthy to govern over us and be the public face of so many hard-working people who do all the shit that Joe Public takes for granted.'

All fair points from our correspondent, 'Golden Brown', who concluded, 'Do us a favour and clarify who are the bad guys, 'cos it sure isn't the people on the front line. I understand (and fully support) any grievance with the bureaucratic assholes in charge, but don't taint the rest of us with the same brush. We work damned hard and do our best for wages on the poverty line'.

First things first: while I would agree that many front-line staff in the civil service do not exactly earn a king's ransom, 'poverty line' is rather over-egging the pudding. There's room for improvement for sure, but nobody behind the desk at the Department for Work and Pensions is cold half the week because they can't afford to switch the heating on at home.

Also, with regard to the suggestion that the reputation of front-line staff remained completely unmauled during the making of this book: I have been sent a couple of quite staggering tales of arrogance at the customer-facing end – and some of these are dealt with in the first chapter, Jobsworths on the Front Line. So, sorry about that Golden Brown, but I feel that the worst of your colleagues are giving the honourable and decent majority a bad name which could, in itself, be regarded as just as damaging and obstructive to the smooth operation of services.

Having said that, this book is arranged according to grass-roots principles – that is, from the bottom up – in recognition of the fact that, like all systems of administration, modern bureaucracy works in a trickle-down manner and that the chief mark of the jobsworth is that they are on the bottom and have no one left to oppress but me and you. It works its way up the greasy pole of administration, unloading the blame as it goes.

I would have replied directly to our correspondent with these points but unfortunately, in a played-for or accidental bureaucratic flourish, Golden Brown forgot to leave a functioning email address, and a long and thoughtful 500-word reply bounced off the Hotmail server like a foam ball off a Plexiglas shield. So, in the manner of a claimant seeking to resolve some arcane point of benefit law by shouting at the outside of a Jobcentre, this book should be considered as Golden Brown's detailed reply – a 184-page book in response to a 172-word email. Once you have read this book, I hope you'll agree that that is a fitting response to the red tape, officialdom and bureaucracy within these pages.

PROLOGUE

A tangled history of red tape

In 1872, Thomas Baker, Barrister-at-Law of the Inner Temple, produced a slim volume of invective with the cumbersome title *The Insidious Red Tape Form of Government in England*. Together with a brief seven-page rant about a completely unconnected subject, it amounted to 39 pages of rational and well-argued loathing of what Baker saw as the self-serving wing of the civil service.

'What then is this mighty power?' Baker asks rhetorically. 'The system has, in one sense, been very aptly described as the art of spoiling paper; for the tons of thick foolscap wasted by its votaries in the effort to kill time are incalculable.'

Previously only known for penning a series of lengthy and sober legal texts, including 'The Laws Relating to Burials in England and Wales' (complete, according to the subtitle, with 'notes, forms' and, rather alarmingly, 'practical instructions'), this pithy tirade was a little out of character, but was also, nevertheless, a fine example of what can happen to any one of us when faced with insurmountable obstacles like government departments and intractable bureaucracy. Apart from the slightly archaic turn of phrase, the anachronistic references to Victorian grandees long forgotten and Baker's detailed examples of waste and extravagance in what seems now like Palaeolithic currency, the book could easily have been written last week.

Particularly if last week was, for instance, the last week of an election campaign. The strong – even shrill – libertarian opinions would not be out of place coming from the mouth of almost any 21st-century politician seeking easy votes in exchange for a popular promise. Baker's fascination with the administrative stalemate, nepotism and corruption of his time still ring true today. Indeed, we hear so much about red tape, how it is essential to cut it in government, local councils and the European Union, it may come as a surprise that a government body has already banned it outright.

Actually, that's not quite true. The Stationery Office – set up by the Treasury in 1786 to bulk-buy office supplies for the Crown – did indeed abolish red tape in 1914, but they were far more concerned with tackling supply procurement problems than setting up an Edwardian Better Regulation Task Force. Taking a lead from legal clerks, who had been binding documents together with red ribbon since the 17th century, civil servants had long since tied official papers with red cloth tape. At the outbreak of the First World War the Stationery Office let it be known that there would be no more red tape, as the red dye was manufactured in enemy territory. The phrase lives on, however, along with all the irritation and anger that excessive bureaucracy causes.

If the term 'red tape' has a long legacy, the concept of bureaucracy is apparently timeless. The word has its roots in France and was first used in the mid-17th century by the French laissez-faire economist Jean Claude Marie Vincent de Gournay. Bureau, an office or a writing desk, is taken from the Latin word *burrus*, the green baize cloth used to cover those desks, while the Greek word *kratos*, meaning rule, gives us the –cracy element. If it was literally trans- lated, bureaucracy would mean government by green cloth – subtly different to rule by red tape.

De Gournay became the French Administrator of Commerce in 1751 and coined the term in response to the multitude of official regulations first put in place a hundred years earlier by Louis XIV's Comptroller of Finance, Jean-Baptiste Colbert – regulations that, de Gournay believed, placed an intolerable strain on commerce.

The theme was picked up by author Friedrich Melchior, Baron von Grimm – an ex-pat German living in Paris who took it upon himself to write a series of occasionally trenchant letters to various sovereigns of German states during the latter half of the 18th century. In his letter of 15 July 1765 he writes, 'The real spirit of the laws in France is that bureaucracy of which the late Monsieur de Gournay used to complain so greatly; here the offices, clerks, secretaries, inspectors and intendants are not appointed to benefit the public interest, indeed the public interest appears to have been established so that offices might exist.'

If there is one thing that can be gleaned from these remarks from analytical minds over a period of 250 years, it is that bureaucracy is enduring and that our relationship with it has not changed for a very long time. Indeed, the concept of a bureaucracy pre-dates all of these writers by thousands of years, having first come to pre-eminence in the world's first nation – ancient Egypt, where enormous royal projects like the Pyramids of the Third and Fourth Dynasties required sophisticated tax collection and administrative effort as far back as 2500 BC. But what we think of as modern bureaucracy was invented by the Chinese – specifically the short-lived Qin Dynasty that ruled between 221 and 206 BC and effectively united China. As a method of control, it must have been a success – Qin Shi Huangdi, the first Emperor of the Dynasty, was sufficiently in command of his realm to order the construction of a life-size, 8,000-strong, terracotta army to accompany him in his mausoleum and into the afterlife. Shi Huangdi's tomb complex, complete with a scale replica of the universe that incorporated gems and pearls set in ceilings representing the cosmos and free-flowing mercury for the sea, is believed to have taken 700,000 workers 38 years to complete. The lavish dedication and ornament are testament to his power in this world, power that came not only from military might, but administrative organisation. In his lifetime, Shi Huangdi was responsible for the construction of 6,000 miles of road and 1,000 miles of canal.

The Qin bureaucracy was developed by subsequent dynasties, particularly the Later Han from AD 25 to 220, into a system capable of running the largest country of its time with a population equivalent to 21st-century Britain. Indeed, the greatest surprise is that, having invented bureaucracy, it still took the Chinese another thousand years to invent gunpowder. Perhaps the discovery was in the hands of an executive sub-committee.

Around the same time as the Chinese were experimenting

with blowing one another up, another great bureaucratic civilisation, the Byzantine Empire were perfecting the dark arts of administration. By the 8th century, what was originally the Eastern arm of the Roman Empire was administered by thousands of officials in its capital, Constantinople – present-day Istanbul. Officials at the time differentiated themselves from the lower classes by wearing more elaborate dress – including conspicuously enormous hats. There is even a mosaic in the Chora Church in Istanbul from around 1320 that depicts a traditional devout subject – Joseph of Nazareth and the Virgin Mary – in a traditional Byzantine administrative context, that of putting their names down on the census. The official in charge of proceedings – Quirinius the Roman Governor of Syria – appears to not so much wearing a hat, as a large modernist sculpture on his head.

Administration and the church go hand in hand elsewhere – not least because of the link between clerics and clerks. In medieval times most bookkeeping and writing was performed by members of the clergy as they were among the few groups literate enough for the work, hence the term 'clerical work'. Notwithstanding the ancient Chinese, Byzantine and Egyptian empires and dynasties, churches pre-date most governments as power structures. The most powerful of these, the Roman Curia – usually known as the Vatican State – has existed since 1588 and acts as the governmental and administrative arm of the Holy See; in effect it is the Pope's civil service and cabinet rolled into one.

The Vatican has many distinctions that mark it out as rather a modern and efficient state. On the face of it – as befits its internationalist status and global influence – its telecommunications, postal and banking systems are second to none; when in Rome, in fact, you should do as the Romans do and post all your international correspondence via the Vatican Post – it will probably reach its destination several days before packages posted in Italy's postboxes. And nearly everyone will get on well with the Vatican's phone system, where there are no automated announcements, labyrinthine menus to negotiate or canned music to pacify you. Your call really is important to the Vatican and even if the Pope's kicked the Pontiff's Pail, your call will still be answered by a nun within 30 seconds. Godspeed and all that, but then again, there is something a little backward – medieval, if you insist – about a country that provides hole in the wall cash machines that can display instructions in Latin, a nation where very little structural change has occurred for 400 years – a city which almost celebrates how little it ever changes. Indeed, in 1979 there was a perception that it was running into financial difficulties and that some of those difficulties were down to the ancient Roman curia, whose complex procedures were described by those who were unfortunate to run into them as 'Byzantine'. The new Pope, John Paul II, called a meeting of the Sacred College of Cardinals to discuss church business – the first time the Sacred College had met in four centuries. It was no coincidence that the last time the College of Cardinals had been summoned was just before the curia was set up. John Paul was trying to redistribute administrative duties back to the Cardinals. After all, at around 109 acres in size and with only about 558 citizens, it's reasonable to assume that there isn't a lot of administration to be done with regards to the Vatican State itself.

At the same time as the new Pope was rearranging the bureaucracy of the Vatican, two things were happening in the UK that had important long-term consequences for all of us. First, Margaret Thatcher came to power and completely changed the bureaucratic landscape with her instinctive loathing of the civil service, local councils and public administration of all kinds. Part of her answer was to expand the role of quasi-autonomous non-governmental organisations – better known as quangos. Quangos were made up of political appointees, rather than elected officials or career civil servants and are, therefore a new kind of bureaucracy, an unaccountable, unelected bureaucracy – one open to criticisms of cronyism and which, because of the way it opens up the executive wing of government to people who may have conflicting interests or axes to grind, affords opportunities for abuse.

Secondly, as we shall see in Chapter 1, a new form of commercial bureaucracy took off with the introduction of the BS 5750 kite mark, the British standard for quality management. Ironically, given her hatred of red tape, Thatcher was a keen advocate of the BS 5750 – seeing it as the British equivalent of the Japanese Miracle – and her Department for Trade and Industry ruthlessly pimped it to the world, despite concerns from business leaders and managers about the extra bureaucracy involved and what many saw as its low value. In essence, the BS 5750 was merely an exercise in validating your processes simply by writing them down. Unfortunately, for such a simple process, it became a self-perpetuating system, where companies who had qualified for it insisted on dealing only with other kite-marked firms. It gave life to thousands of consultant businesses – so-called certification bodies feeding off a system more akin to a pyramid scheme than a philosophy of management. In one celebrated case, Oxford City Council actually insisted that Morris dancers had to be registered for what has been termed 'son of BS 5750', the International Standards Organisation's ISO 9000, in order to take part in a local festival promoted by the council. Because it was an official body, the council could not hire any person or firm, including a group of Morris dancers, unless they were ISO 9000 certified.

Margaret Thatcher's government, who sold the International Standards Organisation (ISO) the BS 5750 and added silliness to the official list of British exports, is therefore directly responsible for the growth of unimaginative, by-the-book, jargon-laden business consultancy that adds little value and makes business less efficient. Unwittingly, as she severed each head from bureaucracy in the public sector, the hydra grew stronger in her beloved, previously efficient private sector. In that way, at least, all those election eve promises, rants and raves about red tape and Better Regulation Task Forces are utterly pointless. All good intentions come to nought. Bureaucracy will never die. Red tape is here to stay.

CHAPTER 1

Jobsworths on the front-line

*Tales of tax, VAT, the Jobcentre and an army
of bureaucrats who only obey orders*

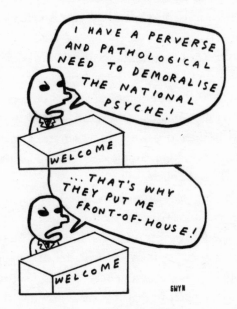

In a side street, not far from the burning Palace of Justice, yet out of the way, stood a man sharply distinguished from the crowd, flailing his hands in the air and moaning over and over again: 'The files are burning! All the files.' 'Better files than people!' I told him, but that did not interest him; all he could think of was the files. ... He was inconsolable. I found him comical, even in this situation. But I was also annoyed. 'They've been shooting down people!' I said angrily, 'and you're carrying on about files!' He looked at me as if I weren't there and wailed repeatedly: 'The files are burning! All the files!'

The Torch in my Ear, Elias Canetti
Translated from the German by Joachim Neugroschel.

Laurence Peter, co-author of the ground-breaking 1969 study of hierarchies, *The Peter Principle*, observed that employers and managers that are competent assess employees according to their results – in other words, their output is what is important. Incompetent bosses, however, take more notice of inputs and how their employees respond to the job's rules, procedures and policies.

Despite being written almost 40 years ago, it clearly explains the success of what we think of as a modern phenomenon – the jobsworth. A similar, but trans-Atlantic term for members of an organisation who blindly obey orders, no matter what the consequences are, is sheepwalkers, but jobsworth is better in that it is an utterly British concept.

So how did the jobsworth become such a British institution? Although the word – a contraction of 'it's more than my job's worth – is relatively modern, having been popularised by the BBC television programme *That's Life* during the 1980s, the tradition goes to the very root of the same obedient

British soul that makes us expert at forming queues and taking orders from anyone in authority, regardless of the actual uniform they are wearing. The same innate character traits could perhaps even explain the success of 1950s seaside prisoner camps like Butlins – it's all there, the discipline of having a day of activities laid out for you, the oppressive, chain-link fences and observation towers and a battalion of redcoats. Like the army, but with lilos.

In Britain, we like our hierarchies, it helps us know where we stand. It used to be the class system, which was ruled over by a believed-in-for-the-sake-of-decency God who dispensed the honour of being the monarch by a divine accident of birth, but now it is an intricate system of power struggles, each layer holding sway over the lower order and, in turn, subjecting itself to a higher bureaucratic power. In our daily life, most of us have ended up at the bottom of this particular structure and the layer just above us is the jobsworth.

A rattling good conversation

'A few years ago,' writes Tim, 'I was introduced to a friend of a friend at some kind of function or another. The trouble was that my new friend was a man who could easily bore for England. Not only that but after half an hour in his company I was convinced that, if ever called upon to do so, he could represent the entire planet at the next Galactic Olympics of the Tedious Arts.'

'He was an exceedingly warm and pleasant man,' confides our correspondent, 'a fact which just served to make his crippling dreariness all the more cruel but also, all the more efficient. Even more unfortunately for all of us, he was also an expert in the field of Quality Assurance Management, which turned his everyday acute tediousness into a kind of short-range tactical weapon.'

Tim goes on to describe the most boring man in all England as 'in possession of a humdrum force field', one which, apparently, 'repelled all exciting topics of conversation and general thrillingness away from him, while simultaneously sucking all the joie de vivre from the air'.

'What I learnt was that not only was quality assurance the buzzword of the moment, it was also the basis of the British Standards Institute's BS 5750. This was back in 1987 when, it turns out, the government was desperately trying to export the standard to the world,' writes Tim. 'The problem was that not only was it a potentially dry subject for conversation, but it was also a completely flawed concept. It was all about conforming – or in the double negative parlance favoured by tedious people, "preventing non-conformance" – and that was more important than doing things better.'

Tim adds, somewhat disturbingly, that 'The BS 5750 was later superseded by the ISO 9000', and while this is absolutely correct, you cannot help but fear for his mind.

The British Standards Institute (BSI) and its famous 'kite' mark have long been symbols of safety and quality. The kite mark itself was emblazoned proudly on products that had passed rigorous tests in design and construction. In my own childhood, I can distinctly remember how the kite mark found its way onto everything from an Etch a Sketch to a lavatory bowl, from a 13 amp plug to a radiator valve.

Without inflicting the same crippling levels of tedium on the proceedings, I should explain more fully just what a BS 5750 was. Stay with me, if you will, and try to ignore those feelings of tiredness, those heavy limbs and the desperate need for slumber. The BS 5750 was a new kind of mark, one which encouraged firms to write down all their processes in 'manuals', thereby – and this is a genuine criticism of the scheme – encouraging all employees to work solely 'by the book'. There were arguments at the time that this had the effect of stifling creativity and also that it made no distinction between productive and counter-productive methods, just as long as they were all written down. It was simply a reward for the otherwise pointless effort of describing everything. It says a lot that when the BS 5750 went to a vote of the International Standards Organisation (ISO), the two countries that offered the most resistance to it are the nations generally regarded as being leaders of industrial quality and efficiency: Germany and Japan.

That day in 1979 when the BS 5750 was launched was the day that the means to an end definitively became an end in themselves. Without even knowing it, the BSI had bestowed a kite mark upon the jobsworth and demonstrated that following rules was just as important as actually making or doing things well.

If you don't eat your beef, you can't have any pudding

Tony tells us of a tale of the worst kind of jobsworth – one who is unaware of their talent for making simple things difficult. 'Back in the mid-Eighties,' he informs us, 'I worked as an agency nurse at Guy's Hospital in London. As an agency worker, you often got the last dinner break on a back shift, ending up in the canteen after almost everything had gone.'

'On one occasion,' reports Tony, 'the Sunday menu had been a choice of either roast lamb or roast beef with Yorkshire pudding.' Tony ordered the beef, only to be told that the beef was sold out. Not faced with a lot of choice, he had to have the roast lamb instead but, 'Noticing a lot of Yorkshire puddings still piled up in the trays I asked if I could have some of this as well.'

'You can't have it with the lamb – it's only sold with the beef,' the server snapped.

Our correspondent thought the serving lady was pulling his leg and laughed out loud.

'But you haven't got any beef,' he offered.

'Doesn't matter,' she replied, 'we can only sell it with the beef.'

Our man was so stupefied it took him a minute or two to move on. Still touched by an unaccountable sadness about the incident, he still gets 'flashes of all that Yorkshire pud rotting in the bin'.

Bad reception for TV detectives

It is an almost universal experience of living in Britain that the people who are responsible for enforcing television licences – the TVLA – are joyless automatons. They, and their specially equipped vans with rotating roof-mounted antennae, are as welcome in your street as a polygraph machine in the Houses of Parliament. One acquaintance of mine used to bury his TV in the back garden whenever reports of nearby vans reached him – something of an over-reaction, perhaps, but indicative of how much fear the vans attempt to spread.

But the worst thing about the TVLA is that not one of them has the imagination to understand why anyone would choose a life without video edification. So much so that even when you repeatedly tell them you do not have a television and are therefore unlikely to be caught with one, they still feel the need to underline that it will all end in tears if they catch you in flagrante with a remote control in your hand.

Two separate accounts follow that highlight the differences between engaging the forces of bureaucracy and trying to ignore them. As you will see, the difference is hard to perceive, except for our second victim who now has a slightly higher phone bill than the first. This is the mark of a true bureaucracy – whether or not you engage with it does not matter, it has satisfied an internal process and just carries on to its next hapless victim.

The space where the TV was

'Having staunchly declined several opportunities to obtain a TV licence – I don't actually have a TV and I refuse to phone them to tell them I don't have one,' writes Howard with an amount of resolve proportionate to the task in hand. 'Who does one phone to report, I wonder, that one does not possess a car or a freezer,' continues our man. 'I finally replied to one of their threatening missives. Apparently, licencing vans were to be patrolling "in your area soon" so I invited them to come around and have a cup of tea, suggesting that together we could look at the space where the TV had once stood.'

After several more reminders and a change of address, a representative then called on Howard. 'He barged past me into the house and then left abruptly, informing me that there was no TV and that we would be "left alone for three years or so".'

TV Cops

'Having not watched the dross belching from my television screen for many months,' writes our next TV licence refusenik, Evi, 'I figured it was a waste of time hanging on to the set. This left me with two months to run on my TV licence, on the reverse of which was a suggestion that I might be entitled to some kind of refund.'

Evi then wrote to the powers that be and explained his situation, only to be told that no refund was available as they can only be given in periods of three months.

'I swallowed that with a little indignation, but hey – I wasn't going to get all worked up for £20.'

Within a couple of weeks Evi received a red letter. 'The letter told me that my house was registered as having no TV licence (as if I didn't know) and I had seven days to ring and explain. Failure to do so would result in my details being passed on to their Orwellian-sounding "enforcement officers".

'I was getting annoyed. I had already explained my situation adequately by mail, so why should I write or ring to explain again? It would all cost me money and they had already had £20 out of me for nothing.'

Evi swallowed his annoyance and rang the number. At the other end of the line was someone who seemed to be briefed to treat all such calls with extreme scepticism.

'Why are you ringing this number?' the man from the TVLA asked.

'Because I was asked to by letter,' replied Evi.

'What letter?'

'A red letter, asking me to explain why I have no TV licence.'

'OK, why haven't you got a TV licence?'

'Because I don't own or have on my premises any receiving equipment, so I don't need one,' explained Evi, as plainly as he could.

This didn't seem to be enough for TV Licence Man. 'If you have got any equipment …'

'I just said I don't …'

'And I just said if you have got any equipment …'

'I just said I don't …'

The Licence Man persisted: 'And I just said if you have got any equipment and receive any broadcasts, you will be liable to a fine of up to £1,000. We will be sending someone round to your house to check if you have any equipment.'

Evi was reaching the end of his tether. 'I wrote to tell you I have no TV, I have now rung to tell you I have no TV. The fact is clear: I have no TV. I am not worried about you fining me, as I am doing nothing wrong. Goodbye.'

'They sent me a letter saying that someone would call at my home to check whether or not I had any means to receive specific broadcasts. If that person was satisfied that I had no such means, then I would be left alone for three years, after which time the process would begin again.'

'Now hang on a minute,' Evi notes with irritation, 'my home is my home – I don't want some great lumbering gorilla rummaging around for a television I haven't got. Why should I be treated like a criminal when my only crime is to loathe watching TV?'

When a Tax Man attacks

Once upon a time, a man we shall call Dave had a lorry. Dave was Value Added Tax (VAT) registered. Unfortunately, Dave had to stop trading because of a family matter and promptly informed the VAT people in the proper way – just as it explained he should do on his VAT registration certificate. Having satisfied all the legal requirements, he stopped working halfway through January and closed the books at the end of February. This enabled Dave to clear all the accounts, get paid by his customers and pay his creditors for fuel and other supplies.

The people at HM Customs and Excise sent Dave a letter ending his VAT registration because he was no longer trading. Simple.

Unfortunately, because he had to stop working so quickly to look after his four children, Dave still had a lorry to sell. A lorry that had cost him £63,000 for the tractor unit and £19,000 for the sliding trailer. Both were less than one year old, but £46,000 was the maximum amount he could get for them. Five weeks after the books closed for trading, the lorry and trailer were sold – for almost exactly what Dave owed on them.

By the first week in April, it was all wrapped up: everybody was happy, all paperwork was witnessed, signed and sealed and everything was completely above board. Dave heaved a huge sigh of relief.

He heard nothing more of it for four whole months. In August of the same year he returned from two weeks camping with his children to a substantial pile of letters on the mat, including one that contained an unwelcome communication from Her Majesty's Customs and Excise. The letter from the VAT people told Dave that he owed them the VAT on the £46,000 sale of his lorry. Suddenly, out of nowhere, he owed the Customs over £8,000.

Dave immediately phoned them to remind them that they had cancelled his VAT registration, as per the rules, and that he hadn't charged VAT because he wasn't allowed to charge

VAT – he was not registered when the truck was sold.

This is when Dave found out that the one thing that government departments and agencies can't stand is someone who applies their own rules against them. Using their almost unlimited powers of superhuman awkwardness, the Customs and Excise then retrospectively registered Dave with a temporary certificate for the two-week period that he sold the truck in, and gave him a month to pay it.

Dave explained to Customs and Excise that he had stopped trading because he had lost his wife and had four children to look after. He had complied with all their rules yet was still faced with an out of the blue demand for over £8,000.

He was determined to resist paying but, in a conversation with a Customs and Excise official was told that proceedings would be taken against him to recover the unpaid VAT. The official explained that Dave's home was at risk. The official didn't actually say that he didn't care about the four children, but the evidence pointed to the true mark of the bureaucratic jobsworth, and Dave couldn't help feeling that the VAT official cared a lot more for the procedural niceties of tax accountancy. In fact, when Dave asked the Customs officer why he was taking this line – his reply was simple: 'Because I can.'

With his back against the wall, Dave contacted the haulier he sold the lorry and trailer to in order to persuade him to stump up the VAT due. After a lot of phone calls and worry, he managed to persuade HM Customs and Excise to agree that the buyer could make a late payment.

The new owners of Dave's rig agreed to make a claim via a VAT invoice Dave sent him – this is the way VAT works; the haulier wouldn't necessarily be out of pocket by paying VAT on purchases like Dave's truck if he could offset it against tax he owed to Customs that he had collected through his sales.

He sent a VAT invoice to the buyer, who then claimed it back. The VAT people allowed the claim, so reducing the VAT paid by him that quarter.

What makes this story of sociopathic bureaucracy a particular favourite is that nobody was the richer. Indeed, it can be argued that everyone that Her Majesty's Customs and Excise dragged into this debacle was poorer, themselves included – the administration involved in chasing payment and then passing around £8,050 is not a trifling matter and the whole affair contributed precisely nothing to the Treasury's coffers. The sum of £8,050 was sent to Dave, who sent it to Customs and Excise, who then deducted it from the VAT that the buyer of the truck owed. It was merely a paper exercise instigated by some pencil-faced bureaucrat who decided that he would be a stickler for the procedural etiquette. It was as if HM Customs and Excise were employing one man to dig a hole and another to fill it in. No money actually changed hands; it was all just a waste of time.

Only obeying orders

While it is true that some of the laws passed by governments are inflexible, others are badly written and a few are just too bloody silly for words, we accept that among all the authoritarian dross and dreary regulation seemingly passed on a daily basis, a number of laws are borne out of a need to address a serious situation or to right some terrible wrong.

Some rules and regulations, however, come screaming out of nowhere as a response to some phantom menace, while others are cooked up by politicians in an attempt to appear macho and not the bloated marshmallow prats we all instinctively feel they are.

One such misguided law was the Computer Misuse Act, 1990. Though it sought to specifically outlaw hacking – and defined it as the use of a computer without the owner's consent – it forgot to define what a computer actually was. Technically, it is now illegal to programme your best friend's microwave oven without checking with him first.

However, the very worst rules become fashionable when some random outrage or another inspires a general mood of 'something must be done' in the media. The Dangerous Dogs Act, 1991, for example, was spawned in a fit of media-inspired political panic after a spate of fatal dog attacks. The Act prohibited the ownership of four types of dog: the pit bull terrier, the Japanese tosa, the dogo Argentino and the fila

Brasileiro. Something had to be done, so God-like in its omniscience, and therefore immune to the existential dilemma of doing so, the government simply banned them from existing. Widely regarded as a badly written law from day one, the Dangerous Dogs Act came back to bite its political masters repeatedly because of the impossibility of its wording – distinguishing, as it did dogs by 'types', rather than breeds.

It should never come as a surprise, then, when any brand new, zero-tolerance policy is drawn up in such a reactionary lather and ends up on the statute books as the latest case of drive-by legislation.

But it always comes as rather a depressing surprise when real people start to do the same thing. When people have become a little deluded by a whiff of power, no matter how trifling, they can start to exhibit knee-jerk reactions and even make up rules and regulations of their own. Governments have an excuse: they are formed from groups of deeply flawed sociopaths and egomaniacs with borderline personality disorders. Normal people are different surely.

Well yes, but unfortunately many normal people are easily led astray by the mirage of authority and end up obeying orders if it means that they themselves can then exercise the tiniest mote of power. So it is then that, even though it has not quite fallen foul of Parliament yet, the current menace of society, the scourge of all that is decent appears to be an item of clothing, irrespective of who is wearing it and whether or not they are remotely dangerous.

We are, of course, not only talking of the hoodie, but also of the baseball cap – the headwear of choice for all clubbers, Home Counties weekend rebels, simpletons and silage dispersal operatives. It's all a question of context though, is it not? A matter of where you draw the line, perhaps.

Sporting chance

For 61-year-old Corinne Chapman of Sittingbourne in Kent, staff at the Vineyard pub crossed that line by asking her if she would tuck away the hood of her pink cardigan if she wasn't going to take it off, citing the oft-repeated phrase that rules apply to everyone. Clearly struggling to draw a new line in the sand, but obviously open to the fact that something wasn't quite right, staff spontaneously rewrote the rules and retrospectively decided to allow the top because 'it was not sportswear'.

According to a statement issued by the Vineyard's propietors, 'Corinne Chapman was never asked to remove her top or asked to leave the pub. She is welcome back at the Vineyard anytime.'

Boys in the hood

No such luck for 66-year-old Tony Wilson in Preston. He walks with a stick and is a wheelchair user, but that didn't stop staff at the Sherwood pub from asking him to remove his baseball cap, because of 'the rules'. And that little incident may have never come to light were it not for the fact that his neighbour and friend, 81-year-old Clifford Critchley, fell foul of the same rules and was asked to remove his Lancashire flat cap. In winter and, more to the point, in Lancashire. Critchley, a decorated war hero and the victim of a recent stroke, was told by pub staff that they were 'cracking down on hoodies'.

Every now and then an opportunity to quote a spokesperson hilariously out of context is just too good to miss. The mouthpiece for the Mitchell and Butler brewery, which owns the pub, said, 'It gets very difficult to differentiate between hats.'

Still, at least Clifford Critchley got served. While attempting to procure a bottle of sherry from a Morrisons store across the border in Yorkshire, 87-year-old Jack Archer, the former Lord Mayor of York himself, was challenged to prove that he was over 21. A similar fate had befallen an 80-year-old lady the previous week. A spokesperson mumbled something about 'policy' – apparently, everyone buying alcohol gets asked to confirm that they are over 21 regardless of how old they actually appear and, yes, the fact that the legal age for buying alcohol is not 21, but 18.

Having an identity crisis

Nowhere is the pressure on jobsworths to play it by the book more unbearable than on staff required to ask for forms of official identity. In the process of putting this book together, I have had all kinds of identity-based frustration sent to me – including one gentleman arriving here from beyond our shores, who wished to take out a contract for a pay monthly mobile phone. In order to prove his identity, he took along his passport, but that wouldn't do. The junior manager in charge of steering his application through the various bureaucratic requirements would not accept anything less than a UK passport – which without having dual nationality he could not provide. So what else would confirm his identity then, he asked? A sworn affidavit from the Ambassador or consular official of his originating country confirming his true identity? Perhaps a solemn oath sworn on a stack of Bibles by a member of the clergy? No, all of that would be too simple. What they asked for was two utility bills, both showing his name and address.

We live in complex times, of course. When Thomas Cook introduced the first traveller's cheques in the late 19th century, the identity of the gentleman bearing them could be proven by a monogrammed handkerchief. Charming, if a little ineffective, when faced with what we are led to believe are consortiums of clandestine terrorists, hell bent on piloting the planet into inferno of one kind or another, but surely the humble utility bill is not much better.

'Ah, so you would like to open a pay monthly account with T Orangavodamobile, Mr Qaeda? Certainly. May I call you Al? Thanks, but these are security conscious times and I'm afraid that we're going to have to insist on seeing your gas bill …'

Don't say cheese

In 2004, changes to the requirements for passport photos were introduced which make it unacceptable to wear even the faintest glimmer of a smile for border security. When the new rules were introduced, even babies had to comply – a require-ment that was sensibly withdrawn two years later after over 15,000 child passport applications were rejected in the space of just ten weeks. One photo was rejected because a baby girl's mouth was open and another mother was told that her 11-week-old child's face was too shiny and she should put make-up on to make the baby's face less reflective.

Children have been required to have passports, instead of the hitherto more sensible option of being included on a parent's documents, since 1998. The policy established, however, there's still plenty of latitude for confusion over who is responsible for filling it in. One case that springs to mind involves Graham, a retired headmaster who was asked by Tabitha, the daughter of a neighbour, to countersign the passport application of her six-month-old son, Brian. Reading the instructions, Graham added his details and signature to section 10 of the form and signed the back of the baby's photograph. He was, therefore, very surprised to have a letter from the Passport Service asking him if he could confirm, to the best of his recollection, that when he countersigned the document, six-month-old Brian had fully filled in and signed the form. They even enclosed a photograph of Brian to confirm the identity of the person who was meant to fill in the form. Graham then took it upon himself to challenge the silliness head on, pointing out that he very much doubted that young Brian had had anything to do with the form at all. But none of it mattered in the end because Tabitha's application on behalf of Brian was rejected on another arbitrary ground.

Where credit's due

Tax credits, a top-up benefit paid to people in work or with children, have got their sponsoring department, Her Majesty's Revenue and Customs, into a fair bit of trouble over the bungling way they were introduced. In fact, so troubled was their launch, it forced that rarest of occurrences: a Minister of State making a public apology.

But it didn't stop there. A range of cock-ups then ensued over many years, which meant that the Revenue had to reclaim over £2 billion a year from hundreds of thousands of people who, almost by definition, were in enough need of the money paid to them in error to have spent it already. To paraphrase a slogan from another arm of the Revenue, maybe tax credits can't help but be taxing.

Geoff passed on this tale of how a happy change in his family's circumstances meant that he never needed tax credits again, and how his naive willingness to be upfront about his new circumstances only cost him time and irritation in the end. 'Could I stop them paying the money into my account?' he asks us, rhetorically. 'I must have phoned them five times to get them to stop, but after each frustrating conversation with the call centre – and not one of the last four calls knew anything about any of my previous requests – absolutely nothing happened. The money just kept rolling into my account. Eventually, a year later, the payments stopped and I got a really snotty letter, vaguely implying that I hadn't been 100 per cent honest and telling me I had to pay it all back.'

A perfect tale of procedural high-handedness inspired Sarah from Bolton to get in touch regarding her tax credits and how she ended up dealing with it.

'I received a letter from the tax credit people at Her Majesty's Revenue and Customs,' she begins, perhaps sensing the cold dread that the sentence carries with it, 'to inform me that they had experienced some computer problems and that my credits for the next three months would be paid in arrears by monthly giro cheque, instead of every week, directly into my bank account.

'I had no problem with that – these things happen from time to time,' said Sarah, who obviously has the kind of low blood pressure and sanguine air ideally suited to dealing with idiots. 'However, I began to get a bit testy when the first giro cheque failed to turn up.

'I phoned the tax credit office who helpfully informed me that the cheque hadn't even been printed, let alone posted. They apologised and told me to go to my local tax office for an emergency payment.'

When Sarah got to the office, she explained why she was there. The woman on reception looked her up and down, according to our correspondent, 'as if I'd stuck a cold turd under her nose'.

That kind of look always speaks volumes, but the woman on reception decided to expand on her supercilious, crap-sniffing sneer with, 'I don't know if "self-assessment" means anything to you, *Miss*, but we are rather busy here helping people with more important matters. If the cheque is still missing after ten working days, only then can you get an emergency payment. You'll have to have an appointment.' After a slight pause, she added, 'I can fit you in in three weeks' time.'

Sarah told the woman that she had been instructed by the tax credit people to call into the office.

Without even looking up from her diary, the woman barked back, 'You're obviously not very good at listening are you, Miss? The payment *has* to be at least ten working days late before we can issue you an emergency payment, you *have* to be seen by appointment and we cannot fit you in for another three weeks.'

Sarah informs us that she then 'smiled sweetly' but then appears to have taken the woman behind the desk to task.

'First of all,' Sarah fumed magnificently, 'I am a Mrs not a Miss, secondly I am full-time self-employed – so self-assessment does mean an awful lot to me, thirdly the payment was in arrears and therefore (technically) already four weeks late and finally, if you don't get the manageress over to the desk immediately, I will play back what you have just said to me on my mobile phone, which I have used to record our conversation.'

'It's funny how half an hour later I got my emergency payment,' Sarah reported.

Tax officials taxed by tax form

Alaric got in touch with a story about a local tax enquiry service and a self-assessment form. It's not normally fertile ground for entertainment, but this particular local tax enquiry service and self-assessment form story is different. In particular, it describes a case of such stupendous laziness, it's a wonder that the member of staff concerned was able to get out of bed in the morning, let alone make it into work.

'I created a limited company in 2000 and at the time, was advised that a director and shareholder would probably have to fill in self-assessment tax returns, but that I need not worry, because HMRC would send me one when they wanted me to do it.

'Anyway, apart from a letter in 2004 saying that they might be sending me one, I've never been sent one yet.'

What stimulated Alaric's post was the sudden arrival of a letter and the events that followed. 'The letter said that I had not sent in my 2005/2006 tax return – due in by the end of January 2007 – and demanded that I did so under the threat of fines.'

Alaric went to the local tax enquiry office to get to the bottom of it. 'An assistant there said I'd need to ring the order line to get the tax return form sent out to me and pointed me to a phone in the corner.'

Alaric dutifully rang up the order line where an official at the call centre told our correspondent that they couldn't send out return forms for previous years and that he would have to ask at his local tax office for one. Despite explaining that he was already at a tax office and that an official there

41

had told him to ring the order line, the call centre official was adamant.

'Well, I can't issue one. Talk to them,' she said.

'So I went back to the same person who had just told me I had to ring the order line and explained what they had said at the call centre.'

'Oh, OK, I'll get you one,' she says, and handed Alaric the correct tax return form.

Job lot – a quartet of disappointing Jobcentre experiences

I have, from time to time, been unavoidably detained in the wretched, piss-stained premises of Her Majesty's Department for Work and Pensions – known, hilariously at the time of my detainment, as the Jobcentre – and therefore I know a little bit about precisely how, why and where the faeces hit the rotary air movement facilitator.

For readers who never passed the entry flaps of a 1990s Jobcentre, imagine a sordid, soiled room that smells like old vomit in an ashtray. Visualise, if you will, staff who have had all the compassion vacuumed from their bodies by a nearby black hole of despair and inadequacy. Furnish the walls with advisory posters pushing condescension and authoritarianism in equal measure. Add a large notice board on which a month-old copy of the local paper has been pinned with every instance of the word 'job' highlighted in pink. If by now you are contemplating hurling yourself from a window, be assured that your mood has been predicted and pre-empted by the removal of all windows except for the Plexiglas shields in nearby interview rooms, designed to deflect bullets, knives and the over-arching sense of disappointment and betrayal. Now it's time to meet the claimants.

I should mention at this point that in my time I've used the Jobcentre not only for seeking employment but also for seeking employees, so know a thing or two about its operations. Anyway, I had been signing on while legitimately starting up a part-time business – all the time looking for either a golden opportunity or sufficient critical mass to build up to break free. Things were starting to go well at last: there were a number of paying clients around who seemed to like my common sense approach to their IT problems and just a bit of networking may have actually clinched the critical mass the business needed. However, a golden opportunity had also presented itself – Channel 4 had signed me up to write and lay out part of their Comedy Circuit website.

Armed with all of this superb news, I hardly minded the fact that there was a forthcoming Jobcentre interview, especially not since the impressive portfolio of facts could be organised into a highly presentable way.

However, upon arriving at the Jobcentre, I was promptly

whisked upstairs, out of public sight, for the interview. I was then led into a room and around the corner, past some cubicles, through a door and into another room. This room resembled something like an administrative battery farm – it was clearly an office where the smile was a proscribed expression.

Shown with severe efficiency to a plastic seat of the sort used for oppressing school children, I couldn't help thinking that the Jobcentre was going to be a very difficult audience for my message of unconfined optimism, but I believed enough in the cause to persist anyhow.

The audience, it turned out, was a middle-aged woman clad in a say-nothing beige trouser suit. I immediately launched into an excited, but measured, action plan of two strands – first a proven IT business, second, a strand based on the more ethereal, yet credible, concept of me eventually writing for a living.

The Lady in Beige was shown everything from both sides, including business projections and a thick Channel 4 contract for writing services. She could see the door had opened a little for me, so took it upon herself to slam it shut in a 45-minute orgy of confidence erosion and mealy-mouthed, dead-eyed unpleasantness.

She kicked off by choosing to completely ignore evidence laid before her and performed a range of literacy tests on me. At this point, I'm pretty sure I detected the tic-like flicker of a smile. One of the tests was to fill in missing words and phrases on a sample application form for a job as a cleaner in a block of flats – oddly enough, a job that my wife had seen that very morning in the local paper. The final line of the application form read, disconcertingly in the light of my utterly feasible plan to get out of the mire, 'I hereby _____ for the position of cleaner'. The Lady in Beige then insisted on the form being signed. The missing word or phrase, by the way, was 'apply' and not 'nominate the Lady in Beige to take a running jump and apply'. Sometimes there is a clue in the length of the space they leave you. All the answers were written on the back.

For some reason, once I had been shown the dark under-belly of the Jobcentre, it became essential that I should no longer be permitted to leave the building through the front door. At the behest of the Lady in Beige, an official led me down a series of stairs.

I half expected to be led into some kind of interrogation facility or perhaps an underground cavern dedicated to the pursuit of domination, masochism, bondage and discipline as practised by the civil service, where claimants are whipped senseless by form-brandishing dominatrixes. Fortunately, it was just the car park. It was a full week before I was sure that an accidental hallucinogen had not somehow made its way into my breakfast cereal.

Mind your language

Meanwhile, over in Southampton, Beryl King, who runs a real employment agency – one where actual jobs may be found that do not involve military service or the sale of double glazing on commission only, was having trouble on the employers' side of the Plexiglas divide.

Having seen both sides of the employment service, I can confidently assert that dealing with the Jobcentre can be just as trying for the employer as the unemployed. For one thing, the people selected by the Jobcentre did not count 'dynamic' among their character traits. My erstwhile colleagues and I conducted interviews at a Jobcentre for an afternoon and left a little suspicious that our role was analogous to that of a drain clearance specialist. We came, we undertook a survey and then took the stickiest turds home.

Back in the real employment agency, Beryl King's search for warehouse workers was running aground. Her advert asking for 'reliable and hardworking' staff was rejected by the local Jobcentre as being discriminatory against people who are not industrious. Exactly the same problem faced Pauline Millican when she sought a 'hard working' assistant for the family optician business in Liverpool. Staff informed Mrs Millican that they could not use the term because it was discriminatory.

Up in Walsall in the West Midlands, Jason Pitt and Bill Wood were denied the opportunity to advertise for a 'hardworking and enthusiastic trainee' for their publishing company on the utterly irrelevant and, may we say, offensive grounds that it was discriminatory towards disabled people. 'Commitment and a desire to succeed' also met with disapproval. It was only the intervention of the then Education and Employment Minister, David Blunkett, which finally allowed the advert past the ever-vigilant and, yes, over-enthusiastic, diversity conscious Jobcentre manager, with the addition of the term 'dynamic'.

No such luck for Dominic Speakman, who was looking for a catering manager for the staff canteen at his travel agency. His particular hate crime was to require applicants to be 'friendly', which Mr Speakman believed to be just about the only mandatory qualification for the job.

Most of these stories prompted press releases from a Department for Work and Pensions spokesperson, or equivalent Jobcentre drone, implying that a member of staff was applying rules in an over-zealous fashion. I firmly believe that these reports are the tip of the iceberg, however, and that common sense has officially left the Jobcentre.

Dial 'M' for Jobcentre

Richard supplies an interesting tale of the pursuit of procedure that seems to fly in the face of common sense.

'After I had been job hunting a little while, I decided I needed to sign on until I got a job,' says Richard. 'I went to the Jobcentre and talked to a lady who told me I would need to make an appointment.'

Keen as mustard, our correspondent started the bidding. 'Can I make an appointment then?'

'No, you will have to phone to make an appointment,' the lady replied.

OK. 'So if I phone, where will it go through to?'

'Here,' the Jobcentre lady said.

'So why can't I just make an appointment with you now? I don't have much credit on my phone and when I call I'm on hold for so long …'

'OK,' she said, 'give me your number, and we will call you.'

'I gave my number to the lady. Five minutes after I had left the building I got a call from the same woman who had just told me I would have to phone to make an appointment, phoning to make an appointment.'

So far, so Byzantine, but there was an unexpected hitch. 'Because of renovations at the Jobcentre, my application to receive Jobseekers' Allowance had to be put off for four weeks. In which time, I phoned up to say that I had got a few days' work.

'They phoned me up again and asked me to come into the office and when I turned up, the same lady told me that they had cancelled my claim because I had done more than 16 hours of work, even though I have gone a month without getting any help. I am told I will have to start a new application and that I will have to make an appointment.'

'OK,' I say, 'can I make an appointment then?'

'No, you will have to phone to make an appointment,' the lady replied.

OK. 'So if I phone, where will it go through to?'

'Here,' the Jobcentre lady said.

'So why can't I just make an appointment with you now?'

And so on and so on …

Operating costs

If you were looking for proof that the world has gone mad beyond redemption, look no further than the political hot potato that is the National Health Service (NHS). Driven by centrally set targets and administered as a collection of sealed economies, somebody forgot to ask where the patients fitted in, if the following stories are anything to go by.

Doctors at Ipswich Hospital decided to treat patients more quickly as they had spare capacity going, well, spare. Normally that kind of attitude would be welcomed as efficient and enterprising, but not in the NHS, which now has more managers than beds. Unbeknown to the surgeons, the hospital had entered into an agreement with managers at its NHS Primary Care Trust – the body that funds the treatments on the Health Service 'internal market' – to not treat patients within four months.

The Primary Care Trust then refused to pay for the treatments to the tune of £2.5 million, in effect punishing the cash-strapped hospital, which was already £16 million in debt. As one observer put it, it was a case of one part of the NHS fining another part of the NHS. All for being efficient and set against a policy of the time of buying in capacity from private hospitals, where capacity that exists right under their noses can't be used for accountancy reasons.

Unlike Ipswich, Medway Maritime Hospital is dealing with its spare capacity in a way that managers would probably approve of. Apparently, there are some large hospitals where consultants and surgeons are being paid to simply sit around and twiddle their thumbs.

One such case is at the Medway Maritime Hospital, where consultant gynaecologist David Penman claims he has so much free time on his hands he has taken up Sudoku. Steady on, there's no excuse for that. According to Dr Penman, running virtually empty day clinics does not actually save any money. He still has to have an anaesthetist, technician and secretary to see the one patient he is allowed to by the financial constraints, when he could use the resources to see more from his substantial list. Unable to progress any further with his Sudoku, David Penman resigned his post shortly after he spoke to the press.

Please stop pretending to be alive

Finally, a tale from Antwerp in Belgium, where Christina Lauwers apparently died, but didn't have the good grace to stop moving.

Belgian Central Administration, a bit like the DSS, DVLA and the Home Office rolled into one, provides a valuable service to the whole of Europe, in that it makes every other bureaucracy – even ours – look rather streamlined and svelte by comparison. The country is renowned for its Kafkaesque approach to all matters of paperwork, something that Belgians are only too aware of, so it was a surprise rather than a shock when the Administration wrote to Lauwers' husband in 2002 to cancel Christina's ID card with their sincere condolences on his loss. He wrote back to inform them that his wife was still very much alive.

A few weeks later Christina was blocked from paying taxes because of her official termination and two years later, the Central Administration for the Registration of Vehicles declined her attempt to register a car because dead people don't make the best drivers.

Some people just can't take a hint, can they?

CHAPTER 2

The Letter of the Law

*Tales of traffic wardens, the police
and other legal impediments*

The bureaucrat is not free to aim at improvement. He is bound
to obey rules and regulations established by a superior body. He
has no right to embark upon innovations if his superiors do not
approve of them. His duty and his virtue is to be obedient.

***Bureaucracy*, Ludwig von Mises**

In our somewhat over-regulated world, it may have escaped your attention that there are now a number of things we are suddenly not allowed to do. These are mostly exotic activities such as the importation of Polish potatoes, angling in the Lower Esk or obstructing an inspection of the Adult Learning Inspectorate. All the kind of activity to set any self-respecting vagabond's heart a-quiver, I think you'll agree. Other prohibitions introduced over the last decade or so include the sale of grey squirrels, offering air traffic control services without a licence and the slightly more mischievous act of 'creating a nuclear explosion', which was outlawed as late as 1998 in what I can only imagine was something of an afterthought.

Among all these is a new offence that surely has the least criminal glamour of all: the new misdemeanour of impersonating a traffic warden.

The wardens' tales

It is all a little bit easy, isn't it? The very embodiment of the word jobsworth, after all, has to be the traffic warden – a person hired with authority to enforce what can seem like trifling and arbitrary offences. For instance, there was a case where a car – a prize in a charity raffle that was parked on a wide pavement outside a Cornish branch of Woolworths – attracted the constant attentions of the town's traffic warden.

I'm reluctant to spring to their defence, but being a parking attendant is as thwarted and downtrodden as it is possible to be. The wages are usually disgraceful and, despite the regular ravings of the tabloids, the days of rewards and bonuses for issuing tickets are long gone. In their place is the standard productivity plight of the employee under pressure: be grateful for your shit job, make us lots of money or be fired. On the other hand, there is a worrying proportion of people who have a predilection for peak caps, who enjoy throwing their weight around and take it upon themselves to sprint from the world of reason at the first opportunity.

One story in particular, from 2003, is a perfect example of a jobsworth doing his job rather too well.

Out of control

Asked to clamp down on illegal parking at city centre bus stops in Manchester – parking that causes congestion and rush-hour misery for motorists and commuters alike – an unnamed warden working for contractors Control Plus slapped a £40 parking ticket on a number 77 bus.

According to bus driver Chris O'Mahony, pointing out that the vehicle was a bus and, therefore, had every right to be parked at a bus stop didn't get him very far. 'Passengers who were queuing to get on were gobsmacked when the warden dashed over,' O'Mahony told the *Sun* newspaper. The hapless jobsworth was immediately sent for 'appropriate retraining'.

Meanwhile, one street in Birmingham, controlled by Control Plus, allegedly became Britain's most parking attendant-infested road, with over 5,500 fines totalling £334,000. Demonstrating their desperation to issue tickets on anything that stops moving, no matter what, six of those fines were for a milk float on its delivery rounds.

Control Plus is owned by Central Parking Systems, a subsidiary of the Central Parking Corporation of Nashville, Tennessee. The Corporation's hilarious promotional tagline is 'Parking Just Got Easier'.

On the other hand, it could be argued that parking just became a lot harder in Birmingham, where workers found yellow lines had mysteriously – magically even – appeared underneath their cars and a Control Plus parking ticket stuck to their windscreens. Faced with virtually the same story, Salford City Council were forced to quash Nasser Khan's ticket when nearby office workers caught road-marking contractors and two Control Plus traffic wardens on camera, gathered with intent around Mr Khan's car. As soon as the lines were down, on went the ticket.

The firm have also been in the headlines in London where, in one instance, vehicles were alledgedly lifted off the road to paint in the lines before tickets were issued. In another incident, a moped involved in a collision on the Albert

Embankment happened to come to rest on a yellow line. While the injured rider was being loaded into an ambulance, his twisted steed attracted the attention of a passing Control Plus warden and earned itself a ticket. Previously, out-of-Control Plus wardens descended on a blood transfusion van, parked in its usual spot outside Lambeth Town Hall, on mourners' cars at funerals and on various housing estates in bizarre dead-of-night penalty charge notice raids at 3.30 a.m.

In Edinburgh, where council-employed contractors took over from the infamously spiteful traffic wardens, or 'blue meanies', you would have thought that the people of Scotland's capital were in for a relatively easier ride. Not a bit of it, thanks once again to the rigid and unswerving dedication of Central Parking Systems. The number of fines issued after the first year of CPS control rose by over 70 per cent. One woman received a parking fine in the time it took her to walk to the ticket machine and back. Judith Whitelaw's pay and display ticket was issued at 5.34 p.m. and the penalty charge notice was issued two minutes later, but when she challenged the attendant with this basic fact, the CPS man apparently just laughed.

At least he didn't swear. Parking enforcement operatives who were busy towing away an American family's car for the heinous sin of parking in a residents' permit bay – albeit with an otherwise valid pay and display ticket – told both a restaurateur and a man of the cloth to 'fuck off and mind your own business' when they intervened to calm heated tempers.

Edinburgh has a rich history of bizarre parking enforcement. Previous triumphs of procedure over common sense include ticketing an ambulance and a hearse (both on active duty, as it were), a transfusion service van full of people donating blood and an RAC breakdown truck attending to a call. After five years of horrendous news stories, the council awarded the contract to National Car Parks (NCP) instead. But they're not out of the woods yet, because Control Plus wardens were not the only traffic wardens responsible for bizarre parking tickets.

Trucker's luck

The area of London known as Belsize Park could soon end up as Belsize No Park, if NCP, the contractors appointed by Camden Council, have their way. Passers-by were astonished to see a truck sink into tarmac up to its front axle where, unbeknown to the driver, a burst water main had caused the road surface to subside. They were even more surprised when a traffic warden immediately issued the immobilised vehicle a parking ticket.

Flaming silly

NCP also hold sway in Westminster, where the council had to have a quiet word with their contractor after traffic wardens slapped tickets on three fire brigade vehicles in Piccadilly attending the scene of a blaze. No really. There were flames and everything.

All of which would come as no surprise to Stuart Bourn. His Vauxhall Carlton aroused the interest of Northampton Borough Council's parking attendants shortly after it was extinguished by the town's fire brigade. The vehicle was towed to the kerbside in order to put out flames leaping forth from under the bonnet. Unfortunately for Mr Bourn, the kerb his charred car was pulled to was marked with double yellow lines, and the vehicle was ticketed while he was arranging with his insurers to have it removed.

A fine frenzy

At least all of these incidents, however silly, centred on vehicles that were actually there. Alan Westwood has only been to Stratford upon Avon once in the last two decades, so was surprised when the council sent him a £60 ticket for parking on double yellow lines in the town – especially as he drove a Ford Transit camper van and had never stepped into the Citroën mentioned on the fixed penalty notice.

The 65-year-old immediately contacted Stratford Council to explain that they must have made a mistake, he didn't own the car and didn't recognise the registration plate either, but the council weren't buying it and refused to budge. Undeterred, they sent him a registered letter with 61 pages of evidence – pictures of someone else's car in a town he hadn't visited for the last 20 years, and some illegible paperwork from the Driver and Vehicle Licensing Agency (DVLA) – and increased his fine to £90 in the process.

'There were 61 pages of documents, including all these detailed written-up notes from the traffic warden saying where he'd been for half the day,' says Mr Westwood. 'I said to them that I wasn't disputing that the car in the picture was parked on double yellow lines – it clearly was – but it wasn't my car, never had been, and the number plate of the Citroën wasn't anywhere near the number plate of my camper van.'

Mr Westwood then pointed out, helpfully, that the tax disc on the errant Citroën had run out, hardly the actions of a man trying to evade justice.

Stratford Council continued to treat Mr Westwood like a fine dodger for another six months, threatening him with court and not giving any credence to his claims. Eventually they dropped the case, but Mr Westwood is still waiting for his apology. 'After I wrote to the appeals tribunal, they sent me a letter saying they'd dropped the case – but I don't remember seeing the word "sorry" in there.'

Many, many tales of traffic warden inflexibility were dug up in the course of researching this book – almost enough for a whole book of their own – but it was surprising to discover that a certain amount of rigidity was actually in the job description for some parking attendants. According to a spokeswoman for Birmingham City Council, 'Parking attendants are not allowed to show any discretion, that is why we have an appeals process.'

Well, yes. It is a tough world out there – especially if you are a traffic warden – and you wouldn't want wardens getting bullied into retracting tickets that they properly issued, but the spokeswoman was responding to questions about one particular case in Birmingham that redefines 'discretion' such that she should have said, 'Parking attendants are not allowed to be anything other than obdurate, misanthropic automatons with thousand yard stares and a deep hatred of society.'

Bertha Williamson is a 78-year-old with severe spinal arthritis and a disabled badge for her car. Parking in the disabled bay at Birmingham's Civic Centre, Mrs Williamson accidentally displayed her badge the wrong way up and was fined £60 for failing to display a valid disability certificate.

Driven round the bend

Spare a thought for Kenneth Quirk, the 70-year-old in a year-long struggle with the awkward wing of the Provisional DVLA. Mr Quirk, from Darwen in Lancashire, made five attempts to get a new driving licence as he passed his 70th birthday. While Mr Quirk does not deny that some of the paperwork flying back and forth between him and the DVLA may have been his fault – gifted as he is with an optimistic view of how much common sense is at the disposal of such a bureaucratic behemoth – one instance at least shows how powerful the desperate need to cling to procedure can be. On this occasion, a letter enclosed with the returned form explained that the DVLA were uncertain of Mr Quirk's place of birth. Was it, the letter enquired, Liverpool or Liverpocl?

Mersey dash looking for cash

While we are on the subject of Liverpool, a priceless story of jobsworthiness reaches us from that city. A Lancashire ambulance crew transporting a seriously ill elderly woman from Ormskirk to Chester found itself in a hole in the ground without any money.

To be more precise, the four-strong ambulance crew found themselves at the toll barrier of the Mersey Tunnel, where we can paint an interesting picture of official obstinacy in action.

It turns out that the tunnel used to just nod through emergency ambulances, take down their number plates and invoice the relevant health authority, but the policy had changed, which is why the operator was insisting on his £1.20 to let the ambulance through. Eventually, after about a quarter of an hour and an upsetting case of battery failure that affected some of the ambulance's emergency medical equipment, the crew emptied their pockets and paid the toll.

Nobody had told the Lancashire crew – made up of a paramedic, two nurses and an anaesthetist – that the system had changed, presumably to stop people dressing up as doctors and nurses, hiring an ambulance, kidnapping some poor wheezing old granny and laughing in the face of authority as they dashed past the toll booth cleverly evading payment for a journey through a buried pipe under a northern river. Because someone is bound to exploit a loophole like that.

The crew returned to Lancashire via the Runcorn Bridge.

Cops scotch hopscotch

Relatively speaking, the West Midlands is apparently a very dangerous place to live. It is where the perpetrators of even minor transgressions, if not properly handled, can quickly escalate in the vortices of crime and delinquency to become villains of the highest order. Well, that is, if you follow the logic of the West Midlands Police it is. Alternatively, you might believe that some members of the force, or those issuing their orders, are credulous buffoons.

So, in these days of international terrorist cabals, security paranoia, gang warfare and … (insert tabloid bogey villain of the moment here), what could possibly be preoccupying a modern police force in one of Britain's largest and most cosmopolitan cities? Which incident had West Midlands Police's spokeswoman offering this serious sounding analysis: 'By targeting what may seem relatively low-level crime, we aim to prevent it developing into more serious matters'? What misdemeanour shows such serious potential to corrupt lives and blight the community that not stopping it in its tracks offers an open door to anarchy? No, it's not disturbing the peace or random vandalism. Neither is it petty theft or taking recreational drugs. Move along, also, shoplifting and graffiti, because hopscotch is in the 'hood. That's the answer. That unfathomable game beloved of tween and teen girls is apparently, if not actually public enemy number one, but enough of a nuisance to call the police in to deal with.

Police community support officers (PCSOs) were deployed, as a priority, to attend a street in Halesowen, where two 14-year-old girls had chalked out five hopscotch grids. The PCSOs arrived on the scene following a complaint by a neighbour – a reminder, if one were needed, that behind almost every act of petty policing, there is usually a twitching net curtain, and behind the twitching net curtain there is a cowering imbecile. The police spokeswoman said that they had no choice but to act when a resident phoned to complain and officers would not hesitate to 'respond robustly' to any further complaints received about antisocial behaviour.

The incident – and here I can't help feeling that the word 'incident' glamorises the game of hopscotch unjustifiably – followed hot on the heels of the West Midlands' last policing gaffe, that of locking up three 12-year-old children found guilty of attempting to procure a healthy childhood.

The three friends – also from Halesowen – wanted to build a den. Nearby residents, presumably pumped up with the fear of crime refreshed daily by the paranoid wailings of tabloid newspapers, claimed the children had been vandalising a tree, when in fact the two girls and a boy were only gathering fallen branches in order to build their illicit tree-house. For the imagined offence they were arrested, had mouth swabs taken for DNA and were fingerprinted and photographed. Their shoes were then removed and they were locked in the cells for two hours. After considering whether or not to charge them with criminal damage, officers plumped for a reprimand – the juvenile version of a caution.

'West Midlands Police deals robustly with antisocial behaviour. By targeting what may seem relatively low-level crime, we aim to prevent it developing into more serious matters,' came the police spokesdrone's mantra. Again.

But it's not just West Midlands Police who are pointlessly burdening innocence with guilt. Avon and Somerset are now throwing their weight around, scaring the living bejeebers out of children.

Once again, as four children – this time aged between three and eight – stood quivering in their boots in a quiet cul-de-sac in the sleepy seaside town of Burnham-on-Sea, two police officers took exception to a chalked out hopscotch grid and decided to define it as graffiti. An Avon and Somerset Police spokesman trotted out the by now familiar, but still tiresome, excuse of, 'Officers attended because antisocial behaviour is a priority.'

On my reckoning that's eight children bullied and eight enemies made by being tough on youthful exuberance, tough on the causes of youthful exuberance. No doubt, all of these 'incidents' have aided a centrally set target for clear-up rates somewhere and sends out a clear message that gangs of hopscotch obsessed tweenies should beware the cops have been called.

Indeed, the Police Federation itself – the organisation of rank and file coppers – issued a dossier of many more silly cases that would seem to back this up, complaining that targets were forcing officers to take action against an assortment of trivial cases. It cites a number of daft incidents inflated to criminal activity for the purposes of keeping up appearances on crime clear-ups to the Home Office. In an age of accountancy, it seems the quantity of offences is more important than the quality of policing, as the following examples clearly show.

A man from Cheshire was cautioned for being 'in possession of an egg with intent to throw'.

A woman was arrested on her wedding day in the West Midlands for criminal damage to a car park barrier when her foot slipped onto the accelerator pedal.

A child from Kent took a slice of cucumber from a tuna sandwich and threw it at another child, the parents of whom claimed it was an assault, which led to the arrest of the first child.

Another child from Kent was arrested for throwing buns at a bus.

A man in the West Midlands was cautioned after he threw a glass of water over his girlfriend.

Two children from Manchester were arrested for firearms offences when they were discovered in possession of a toy pistol.

Perhaps it is stories like these which prompted Ian Pointon, the chairman of the Kent Police Federation, to use an open meeting to tell officers that, 'The target-driven culture rammed down our throats by our political masters has focused our attention on ticking boxes and not on quality of service.'

Paperwork cuts inevitably lead to more paperwork

When you ask what is for all intents and purposes a bureaucratic organisation to cut bureaucracy, do not be surprised if it merely moves all the administrators, accountants and pointless management from one office into another. So, while it would be a pleasure to report that the Metropolitan Police are taking the fight against red tape seriously with their proposed new Bureaucracy Minimisation Programme (BMP), it wouldn't take Sherlock Holmes to deduce, or at least suspect, that something else entirely different will happen in the end. In fact, the slightly clumsy name alone should be a good enough indication of the way things are probably going to turn out.

The idea of the programme is to offer a welcoming hand to suggestions on cutting back pointless administration from members of the force, civilian workers and even ex-coppers. On the face of it, a very good idea, but will it ever take off?

Reports from the Metropolitan Police Authority, the public body that oversees the capital's constabulary, cast doubt on its chances. Worse still, they indicate that the programme would be a laughing stock if it wasn't so painful to observe. The BMP has apparently put in place a ten-point process of the stages it requires to accept and carry out suggestions for improvements from all corners of the Yard.

The whole programme is wrapped up in a database, which has the benefit of exciting both IT consultants, because of the money, and politicians, because they will do just about anything to appear 'with-it' and modern. Suggestions are to be logged, given a number and then face an impact assessment designed to test their effect on women, the disabled, minorities, gays and lesbians.

A summary of the report slips into management consultancy-speak with depressing ease, given the stated aim of cutting out the crap, and promises that 'the proposed approach will enable the effective coordination of all activity aimed at reducing unnecessary bureaucracy within the [Metropolitan Police], and provide visibility of respective contributions from established programmes and initiatives while also allowing the commissioning of complementary work in accordance with agreed priorities, where this becomes necessary.'

The report trundles on with organisational flow charts and diagrams, one of which resembles nothing quite so much as an ants' nest under attack. It eventually settles on what it sees as the final shape of the BMP. Long after the laughter has faded we learn that it will be 'cognisant of the NBA's and National Bureaucracy Task Force's findings (as adopted or amended through the NPIA) and also be receptive to validated inputs received through the proposed MPS Ideas & Suggestions Scheme and Organisational Learning Programme'.

Oh, and it will need a dedicated person to run the database and first year costs are expected to be in the region of £50,000.

One final thought on the red tape that apparently takes up so much time in the police force.

No lesser a figure than a former home secretary reported that the officer who accompanies him in public told him that, if there was an attempt on the home secretary's life, he was, '… going down with [the home secretary]. I couldn't face the paperwork, sir.'

Court short

Two new 'super courts' – combined magistrates' and county courts commissioned under the Private Finance Initiative – have proved to be less than super.

The £30 million Manchester court has integrated a stunning glass atrium into the design, but prison vans are unable to drive into the security area for prisoners, while developers of the new £25 million courthouse in Kidderminster had a touching faith in the honesty of its guests, given its function, and did not provide any locks for any of the doors.

The long wait for a lollipop lady as CRB rules suck

When the crossing patrol lady at Seascale Primary School in Cumbria left for pastures new, existing staff member Laura Jackson gamely offered to step into the lollipop-shaped hole.

Quite properly, like anyone working with children, Laura had already been checked and passed by the Criminal Records Bureau and thought everything was in place for her new duties. But she reckoned without the arcane world of the CRB, whose official rules mean that any new role taken on attracts a fresh, identical check – a check that can take from four to six weeks to come through.

Cumbria County Council, meanwhile, swung into action with a helpful letter reminding parents that it wasn't technically the council or school's responsibility to get children to school safely. They also warned teachers that, without the requisite extra CRB check, they were not allowed to plug the gap on a temporary basis.

At the time, Gill Hartley, Head of Seascale Primary, told local paper *The Whitehaven News* that, 'Even teachers can't see the kids across the street – I'm CRB-checked to be a head teacher but not to see children over the road.'

Several weeks later, the school eventually got its patrol, and children could cross the busy village road in safety once again. While the powers that be checked that the member of staff they had already judged as fit to work with children was, oddly enough, fit to work with children, there were immediate and obvious dangers present on a busy village road.

Perhaps it isn't surprising that, with such a fine eye for the small print, the CRB lost sight of the bigger picture: in 2007 it emerged that 27,000 files on foreign convictions were missing from the database while the government and police forces squabbled over a five-year period about whose responsibility it was to add them. In the same five years – perhaps in order to make up the numbers from not operating with a full quota of vagabonds – 2,700 people were roundly turned down for jobs after they were unjustly labelled as criminals, thanks to errors in the CRB database.

The RNLI's street lifejacket

The charity collecting tin is not what it used to be. Subtle pressures from the forces of bureaucracy have made themselves felt in recent years. A Royal National Lifeboat Institution (RNLI) flag-day collector recently bounded up to me dressed, if appearance was a reliable guide, to rescue sailors in trouble adrift off the Faroe Islands and to do it in the down-draught of a helicopter, to boot.

After the money had changed hands, however, he was unable to place the not quite sticky enough sticker onto my lapel. 'We're not allowed to do that anymore,' he said, with the robust nautical boom of a man used to casual chit-chat in the teeth of a North Atlantic gale. 'You'll have to put that on yourself,' he added, 'it's the rules.'

'Really?'

'Yes, really. And I'll tell you what else – you see this lifejacket I'm wearing?'

'Aha,' I replied.

'Well, it's not real. I have to tell everybody I come in contact with that it is not a real lifejacket, as well,' he said. 'It's a bit silly really.'

Indeed.

Out of the frying pan, into the 1996 Food Labelling Act

Another tale of the truth being stranger than fiction variety – as well as a fine example of how the anal retentiveness of an official department can squeeze the last morsel of joy out of the most innocuous situations – comes from Wales. Black Mountains Smokery, a local food company, has been forced by consumer watchdogs to explain that its Welsh Dragon sausages do not contain dragons. Trading standards officers from Powys County Council are advising the smokehouse that it must now include the word 'pork' prominently – as part of the name of the food – in order to avoid misleading customers about their contents.

Pork was already on the list of ingredients, but it appears that that wasn't good enough for at least one member of the public, as the Trading Standards Department were apparently acting on a tip-off. It seems that the Smokery were dobbed in to the authorities for the heinous outrage of contravening the 1996 Food Labelling Act. (This alone opens an entirely new question for us: just how many people are stalking the streets of an average British town like Crickhowell with this kind of highly specialised information?)

Somewhat on the defensive by now, a county council spokesman told the *Western Mail* the following morning, 'I don't think anyone would imagine that dragon meat was being used but we would not want vegetarians to buy the sausages believing they were meat-free.'

Heavens, no. Because, by default, vegetarians always buy sausages without checking that they are suitable first. Good grief.

The naming of the tarts

None of the Dragon sausage fiasco would come as any surprise to Val Temple of the Sgt Bun Bakery in Weymouth. Mrs Temple earned a visit from Dorset trading standards officers after they received a complaint from a member of the public about her food labelling. The reason? Sgt Bun has, for a number of years, made little Muppet-inspired cakes, finished off with marzipan pigs and frogs. Her crime was to call these cakes pig tarts and robin tarts – the frog's name is Robin, apparently. Unbelievably, the somewhat jobsworth Trading Standards department of Dorset County Council took exception to the names because they did not contain any pork or robin and, as for Mrs Temple's other speciality, the paradise slice, that fell foul of the regulations because it 'was not made in Paradise'.

Now Mrs Temple is forced to change the name of her animal-free animal tarts to 'novelty tarts with jam and fondant', which is so bereft of any style, she may as well stop bothering to make the little marzipan animal faces on top while she's at it. Her Paradise Slice becomes 'almond, fruit and nut slice'. Ho hum.

Dorset County Council's Trading Standards remarked with an air of boredom, 'Food must be properly described so consumers can tell what it is.'

CHAPTER 3

Councils of Imperfection

Tales of local authorities with a license to kill fun

The town hall is closed until opening. It will remain closed after being opened.

Open tomorrow.

Sign outside a new town hall to be opened by the Prince of Wales

This site is now open 7 days a week. Closed Wednesdays and Thursdays.
Council tip, East Riding of Yorkshire

There's something about the hapless local council that inspires rage among the temperamentally challenged. Perhaps there's a suspicion that they are getting their noses into more and more areas of our daily lives.

Given that this book is about the quiet insertion of procedure, protocol, rule and regulation into absolutely every facet of daily life – most of which is organised locally – perhaps it's not really a surprise that councils came up time and time again in stories sent in for this book. After all, they have responsibility for education, social services, pub, club and venue licensing, smoke-free enforcement, local highways, planning; you name it, they've got a finger in the pie.

But, as we shall see, because of a certain amount of municipal risk aversion and rather onerous legal responsibilities, some councils seem to have a rather unhealthy tendency to prevail against all forms of fun that are not deemed 100 per cent safe. In particular, their duties under the licensing laws rather cast them as dour old Calvinist killjoys, so it was interesting to see how they fared against a couple of real churches.

Dudley tries but still makes church cross

There aren't many things duller than a planning dispute between the owner of a property and their local council, and there are no prizes for guessing which party usually contributes the most dullness to the proceedings. Occasionally, however, a planning disagreement comes along that paints the local planners in a somewhat brighter light, if not at first glance.

Stepping out of the bright light on this occasion are the planners at Dudley Council in the West Midlands, which leaves the enlightened applicants, Dudley Wood Methodist Church, in the spotlight – or so it would at first seem. The church began to kick up a merry old stink when the council told them they would have to pay £75 for planning permission to site a large freestanding wooden cross in its grounds. According to Dudley Council, centrally set guidelines in place for this kind of thing – rules that they are legally obliged to follow – classify a cross as an advertisement. That is, as far as planning law is concerned, which just goes to show the kind of trouble you get into when you have to start classifying everything. Taxonomy of this kind really starts to resemble Satan's pottery class – that is, the Devil's handiwork.

Officially then, a cross is an advert in the same way that other roadside symbols and signs are. Dudley Council were inadvertently drawing a comparison between a cross and the golden arches, between Jesus and the Little Chef, between the crucifix and those flashing neon arrows you get pointing at lap dancing clubs and other basements of sexual desperation. Given this blasphemy, it is a wonder, nay a miracle, that the Planning Committee were not all turned to their component molecules in a wrathful lightning strike and forced for eternity to bail out the Grand Union Canal with a sieve. Certainly, at this point, and only aware of these facts, I was with the Methodists all the way because, while technically correct, the council were not winning many friends through their crass, cross demands.

But that wasn't the whole story, as it turns out. With the Methodists ready to open their brand new £200,000 replacement house of God, the council saw sense and offered the church an olive branch. Council officials said that, in order to get around the guidelines, the church could choose to classify the cross as a memorial, which would make the planning application free of charge. Presumably, and I am stooping to a guess here, besides offering a free application, planning officials might also have thought that their suggestion would find favour with the church – a memorial, after all, is an object of veneration and respect, a place for the quiet contemplation of others. You can't say that about an illuminated 72-sheet billboard promoting the miracle of clean laundry or gourmet cat food.

A thoughtful compromise then, but the congregation were having none of it and even said they were 'offended' by the idea that a cross could be a memorial. So why were the congregation having so much trouble about calling their cross a memorial, even only for temporary administrative purposes? It turns out that the church were not prepared to compromise because referring to their crucifix as a memorial implied, in their collective mind, that the council thought that Christianity was dead. Well it might not be dead exactly, but it sure smells funny right now.

It is an inescapable conclusion that some people actually enjoy the attention of being insulted – the flock's chorus of bleating indignation was thrown into sharp relief when their Minister, Dr Paul Nzacahayo, told local newspaper the *Express and Star* that the church would rather pay the £75 to submit an application for an advertisement than refer to the cross as a memorial, neatly bringing all concerned straight back to square one.

The new church was eventually opened without its cross. Neither council officers nor members of the Planning Committee were subsequently consumed by the fires of hell and damnation.

There's no smoke without eternal damnation

It's well known by now that you can't smoke in a public building or workplace anymore – in pubs, restaurants, nightclubs, cafes and shopping centres – in fact, any enclosed space apart, in the parlance of the long arm of the law, from a private dwelling and a few designated exceptions. And it is all to be enforced by officials of your local council.

Depending on your view of the habit, the general thrust of the smoke-free zone is either all well and good or a blow to your right to cough like a badger on pseudoephidrine. But there's another aspect of the law that is less well documented and that is the issue of signage. Every smoke-free building, and that, as we have seen, is basically all of them, must display a sign, the minimum dimension of which is A5. The sign is to alert everyone to the smoke-free status of the building and reads 'NO SMOKING' in the typeface possibly known as Authoritarian All Caps, under which it says, 'It is against the law to smoke in these premises'. All of this under the international 'no smoking' symbol, a single burning cigarette enclosed in a red circle with a red bar across it. It is a symbol that perversely reminds me of the utter Joy of Smoking, with its perfect little wisp of graphical smoke curling artfully off the hot end.

Quite apart from the issue of having yet more signs on the wall that start with the word 'No', there are other issues at stake here. For instance, one of the big problems with the new law is how it applies to churches. They are public buildings, of course, and should be subject to the same laws as any other public building. You won't find a member of clergy who has a problem with the new smoke-free status either, and even if you could, when was the last time you saw anyone actually spark up in a church? Precisely, it just doesn't happen, ever, and if it ever did, the person responsible would instantly feel the unspoken censure of a hundred or so morally upstanding, yet polite, people and stub it out immediately. If, heaven forbid, they carried on, they would probably just be tutted to death. It has never happened, and it will never happen, so churches can carry on, much as they have always carried on, smoke-free except for incense and the sweet smell of candles.

The clergy still aren't happy though and that is because they are compelled to put the smoke-free signs on the door of every church and cathedral, under duress of law. Not a nice sign in keeping with their 'premises', say, gouged out of a stock of polished yew or set in a churchy typeface like Rottweiler Blackletter or Merrie Olde Englyshe, but the same efficient sans serif as you'd use at the entrance to an office of the Department for Work and Pensions. Maybe they should just be done with it and rename all the churches Godcentre Plus.

Let's face the music but refrain from movement of a rhythmic nature

Still, who would be surprised if the smoke-free enforcement

officers of your local had been spontaneously struck by lightning from under a wide blue sky and reduced to a little pile of ironic ash? Because local authorities do appear to take our moral welfare very seriously, even if we don't. Nowhere is this more obvious than in the activities of your average local government licensing department – the fine upstanding folk who these days regulate not only alcohol, but music, singing, dancing, frolicking and all permutations thereof.

So, with such a tight control over the forces of wickedness and sin, it should come as no surprise that the moral guardians at Westminster Council decided to get tough on 'swaying'. Bowling up one night in 2001 to two Pitcher and Piano pubs – owned by Wolverhampton and Dudley Breweries – officials witnessed four and then five people 'moving rhythmically' to piped music playing over the bar's PA system. Outraged and disgusted, the council prosecuted the brewery, which was then fined £5,000 and ordered to pay £1,600 costs in addition to its own legal fees, for not having a Public Entertainments Licence – or PEL.

'We have signs up everywhere, managers instruct customers, we turn the music down, rearrange the furniture and so on,' said Derek Andrews of Wolverhampton and Dudley. 'Unfortunately, we can't always stop people acting spontaneously.'

Indeed. Stupid spontaneous rhythmic movement always ruins the orderly, efficient consumption of alcohol for the purposes of amelioration of thirst or the satiation of an urge for intoxication. What's wrong with them? Can't they have fun standing still?

When it became clear that the pubs concerned did not provide a dance floor, nor live entertainment, nor any meaningful encouragement to boogie, the industry paper *The Publican*, representing its confused readers, sought an explanation and definition of what, exactly, constituted dancing. Bob Currie, director of the community protection department at Westminster Council obliged, in a letter.

'Dancing could be described as the rhythmic moving of the legs, arms and body usually changing positions within the floor space available and whether or not accompanied by musical support' – only confirming that, when it comes to the execution of honest, ribald fun, there's nobody more expert than the folk at your local council in killing it stone dead.

The Pitcher and Piano were not the only pubs to feel the cold, clammy breath of Westminster Council's PEL enforcement officers. As part of the same ongoing campaign, two pubs belonging to Fullers brewery were served official written warnings for people 'swaying'.

Wolverhampton and Dudley later applied for PELs for these and other Pitcher and Piano public houses just to make sure that spontaneous dancing by its customers did not get them into trouble again. The licenses cost £7,000 each.

The fingerprint of fun

I barely know how to break it to you, but someone in South Somerset District Council has gone completely mad. In this day and age of lying politicians and spin, all of us are accustomed to the incremental widening of official powers, known as function creep. Yeovil, in Somerset, however, seems to be more interested in function leap, where quantum bounds are being made into your personal liberties.

Yeovil, like Westminster with its surveillance over unauthorised dancing, does not get on with the idea of fun and has pioneered the latest in creepy surveillance technologies to prove the point. The council has installed fingerprint scanners on the doors of many pubs and clubs in the town centre in order to add a further layer of intrigue and suspicion to the simple idea of having a pint. So now, in order to obtain a pint of Crompton's Olde Tumescent in Yeovil, you'll have to go along to some kind of pub passport centre equipped with some photo ID, probably a recent gas bill and, of course, some fingers.

Under the scheme, called InTouch, your prints will then be taken and logged against your ID. At the first hint of trouble you'll be summarily banned from every pub in the town. The Home Office – who despite denying having anything to do with it, bankrolled the pilot scheme with £6,000 of funding – now want to extend the scheme to larger cities like Hull,

Coventry and Sheffield. Many more busybody local authorities are also starting to show an interest.

Though voluntary in its current incarnation, South Somerset District Council has written to local publicans stating that by not installing InTouch and failing to preside over a 'considerable' reduction in alcohol-related violence, they risk having their licenses taken away.

But what of the results? South Somerset District Council released figures that showed a 23.5 per cent drop in alcohol-related crime in the pilot venues, which sounds quite impressive until you realise that the rest of the town – the area not covered by the InTouch scheme – showed a 48 per cent drop in alcohol-related crime over the same period, and that some statistics had shown a rise in domestic violence.

Life's a pitch when you lose the plot

When Circus Mondao rolled into town in north Norfolk for a month-long show – hastily arranged to replace two cancelled shows elsewhere – they reckoned without the 2003 Licensing Act. They also failed to take account of North Norfolk District Council, whose strict compliance with the letter of the law inspires a story of bureaucracy at the absolute pinnacle of madness.

Without time to apply for a full licence, Circus Mondao

had to fall back on provisions in the 2003 Licensing Act which allow for the issue of 'temporary event notices' which in turn meant that the big top could only stay in the same place – or premises as the council insists on calling them, whether they are village halls or fields – for just 15 days.

Given that they were booked into Beeston Regis, near Sheringham, for a whole month, they would potentially have been able to entertain the crowds for only the first two weeks of the month – a disaster for their box office.

North Norfolk District Council, however, rode to the rescue with an idea they appeared to be feeling really rather proud of. The field – sorry, premises – in which Mondao had pitched their big top, had a track that ran through it, explained the council, with what they may have imagined was a daredevil, anarchic flourish. Technically, this meant that it was two fields … err, premises, and not one. All that the circus had to do was to move themselves from one side of this track to the other, halfway through their run.

To put that into context, 'all they had to do' after their last show on the old site was spend two and a half hours taking the big top down only to spend another seven hours re-erecting the tent just 50 yards away on the other side of the track. In the meantime, they had to move everything else – tents, animals, box office, trucks, the whole kit and kaboodle – along with the big top.

An exercise in futility at best, and all in pursuit of an issue of technical etiquette, because it transpires that the only people that the Licensing Department at North Norfolk District Council had to fear by turning a blind eye to the regulations, was the Licensing Department at North Norfolk District Council. They had cunningly exploited a loophole in the 2003 Licensing Act, which was responsible for several people wasting a ten-hour day of pointless and soul-destroying toil in order to prevent them from taking legal action against themselves.

Tony Gent, licensing team leader at the council told the *Eastern Daily Press* that, 'This was the best result I could come up with at such short notice,' ignoring the fact that the best that anyone could have done was absolutely nothing at all.

No joy allowed at the ministry of fun

It was not only in Norfolk that the 2003 Licensing Act made its presence felt – the new regulations had a profound effect on national levels of jollity throughout the country during 2006. Far from the free-for-all National Binge Drinking Olympics we were promised as a result of the introduction of the *outside possibility* of 24-hour pub licensing, all manner of encumbrances to having a good time cropped up instead. Dozens of carnivals, fetes, centuries-old traditions and exciting new ventures already under threat through spiralling insurance premiums and the insane ramblings of health and safety consultants, were squashed under the dour new provisions of the Licensing Act.

The Act replaced 22 existing Acts of Parliament and made changes to over 60 more in England and Wales. It also left some existing legislation curiously orphaned in Scotland, including, apparently, the 1952 Hypnotism Act. Its stated intentions were to simplify alcohol and entertainment licensing, to free up licensing hours and lump the whole lot away from Magistrates' Courts and onto local councils. Job done.

Steered through Parliament by the so called Ministry of Fun (the Department for Culture, the Media and Sports), the 2003 Licensing Act is what happens when you really have nothing left to legislate against – the right to protest, have a fair trial and various breeds of dog have all come under attack so far and the government is now forced to have to stamp down on different sorts of fun instead. Can we now confidently expect a new law to tackle the menace of Bakewell tarts and hot buttered crumpets any day soon?

Although the outcome of the Act made it appear as if a party of fundamentalist Calvinists were roaming the land wagging their fingers at people enjoying themselves, the real root of what happened was that it was just another of those badly drafted laws; worse still, it was a badly drafted law that regulated at the meeting point of clashing cultures.

On the one hand is the world of politics, of podgy, mono-maniacal wonks who would regulate anything – no matter what the consequences – purely in aid of the brief moment that their eminently kickable faces can enjoy the spotlight.

(As an aside, brace yourself, if you will, and watch almost any self-conscious politician letting their hair down on television, then reassure yourself that it isn't such a mystery that they would like to effectively ban as much dancing as possible because they clearly have no talent for it.)

On the other side of the equation is everybody else and the hapless middlemen – the bureaucrats neatly inserted to carry the can and deflect the blame from crap legislation, while struggling to interpret their way through the miasma of exemptions and exceptions which, like any attempt to codify and classify different types of joy, are bound to fail.

The 2003 Licensing Act, together with the guidance notes that sprang from it, appear to exempt many things from being classed as licensable, among them Morris dancing, public information films, religious services and performances that take place at garden fetes, as well as entertainment that is performed on a moving vehicle; which brings me on to the next case – that of the disappearing carnivals.

Attention: illegal pom-pom

Apparently there are just too many Trowbridge Majorettes and they do insist on twirling their batons and punching their pom-poms in the air. For these outrageous displays of frivolity, and despite 30 years of participation, they will not be performing at the Trowbridge Carnival ever again – not unless the carnival stumps up £2,000 for a licence that is, or West Wiltshire District Council, the local authority responsible for licences in Trowbridge, stops being silly, and that could take a take a little while based on the evidence thus far.

Someone at West Wiltshire District Council's Licensing Department must have a grudge against Majorettes – we can only imagine what pom-pom-based slight has so warped the council it appears to be making up laws to exclude them from the Trowbridge Carnival – but it must run deep because there is a determined and literally no-nonsense attitude at work in the council.

The problem, apparently, is that majorettes are dancers, and unlicensed dancing and frivolity is forbidden and will not be tolerated under any circumstances. Not everyone has the same problem, however. The organisers of Notting Hill Carnival managed to grant exemptions for masqueraders walking and dancing in front of their floats by drawing a comparison with Morris dancing, which is exempted. In Somerset, where a thriving and colourful carnival scene attracts hundreds of thousands of spectators, licensing authorities avoided imposing unnecessary requirements on organisers. West Wiltshire was different, however. Clearly apoplectic with fear at the thought of 30 eight-year-olds twirling their batons through the mean streets of Trowbridge, they appear to have acted unilaterally, so far as we can tell, by making up yet more rules in order to stop it.

The council appear to have gold-plated what rules there are in existence already by coming up with another: the 50 per cent rule. West Wiltshire's new rule states something along the lines of: carnivals do not need licensing where the total number of people on foot is less than 50 per cent of the total number of floats. We say 'something along the lines of', because no comment about the rule or where it had come from was forthcoming from either West Wiltshire or the Department for Culture, the Media and Sports. It does not appear on either of the organisations' websites and spokes-people and PR officers seemed strangely reluctant to be drawn into any conversations about it and would not answer any emails on the matter.

To put the 50 per cent rule into context, 60 floats is an enormous carnival and 30 majorettes do not maketh a disco.

Time machine, gentlemen please

Albert Einstein once famously remarked that 'only two things are infinite, the universe and human stupidity, and I'm not sure about the former'. He also said that 'bureaucracy is the death of all sound work' so, whether or not he had a lot to say about time, space and the universe with his theories of special and general relativity, I for one would still be the first to grant him the status of genius.

There are, however, moments where his considerable genius for science would appear to intersect with his special knack for one-liners on the subject of human folly. On the subject of time, for example, he perceptively noted that the only reason for it 'is so that everything doesn't happen at once'. His Special Theory of Relativity showed that time is a relative thing and not nearly as immutable and fixed as our feeble senses perceive it to be. He even proved that if you travelled quickly enough, it was possible to slow down time – but it seems that that isn't good enough for the good burghers of Norwich, who, it turns out, expect residents to be able to travel back in time in order to fulfil their civic rights and responsibilities.

It is not every day that a local council is found operating contrary to accepted scientific thinking on the nature of the universe, but word has reached us that officials at Norwich City Council found themselves in just such a curious position while inviting objections to late licences in city centre pubs.

The council wrote to residents in the Nelson ward of the city to invite them to raise objections to one particular local hostelry's application for a late licence. The letter was sent out on 28 July and the final deadline for objections was 23 August. But then the council realised that they had inadvertently given the wrong date for objections on the letter, so they moved the deadline back to 23 July, therefore creating a period of minus five days in which to both have the letter delivered, and for residents to be consulted on their concerns.

Not surprisingly, residents were unable to get their objections in by the official date because, even in a forward-thinking city like Norwich, an appropriate vehicle capable of velocities in excess of the speed of light, along with the requisite wormhole in the space-time continuum was, oddly enough, unavailable. What is perhaps not quite as strange is that Norwich City Council stuck rigidly to the letter of the law and refused to consider objections that were received in time for the published deadline, but were received later than the official one, which was because of the unfailing genius of the council, all of them. The pub received its late licence with no objections. Two other pubs in the city appear to have also gained late licences as a result of the immutable laws of physics. At the time of writing, no wormhole has been sighted in the vicinity of Norwich.

Cambridge's infinite loop spam

The city of Cambridge may be famous for its general air of intellectual achievement, bestowed upon it by the presence of a world-class university, but the law of compensation also applies – where there is erudition and intellect in gigantic proportions, there must therefore be an equal amount of the thick and the fatuous at large. Fortunately, this dichotomy is usually confined to the student body, with opposing qualities even evident in the same student body – as anyone in town after the finals will see, it is not uncommon to witness spectacularly gifted double firsts running around with underpants on their heads. Still, if you're looking for 'stupid' you would always be well advised to take a glance at the fields of public bureaucracy and IT and in the next case, an unholy alliance of the two.

Cambridge City Council and a recipient of one of its emailed invoices inadvertently let loose a blizzard of spam on 200 businesses in the city, forcing many to spend hours downloading the same invoice thousands of times. The council fessed up to the problem, while honourably admitting it had no idea what the cause was. However, there was speculation that a glitch at the council office end, where the original mails were sent several times, was exacerbated when the email server of one of the invoice recipients suddenly went berserk and started replicating the message and bouncing it out to all and sundry on the circulation list in a recursive fashion known as an infinite loop. The result was that some businesses reported a thousand incoming emailed invoices per hour and utter chaos.

Sent to Coventry – but nobody tells the drivers where to get off

More pointless reiteration, this time in the West Midlands, where Coventry City Council has apparently invented an infinite loop of their own – the never-ending roundabout. This is Coventry's interesting and rather avant-garde road junction – a traffic signal-controlled roundabout where all left turns have been banned. Technically – and what are the city's transport managers if not absolute technicians – this means that, having lured unsuspecting motorists onto the junction, the council will never allow them to leave and they will presumably be forced to orbit the roundabout until either they run out of fuel or they become faint with dizziness. The council hastily covered up the signs after a driving instructor drew their attention to the embarrassing gaffe.

Bus fails to stop at bus stop

Not really the most fascinating headline in the world but, as I know to my personal disgruntlement, they don't always stop even when it's pissing down with rain and you are virtually star-jumping across the road to draw attention to yourself. You star-jump because you know they are not going to stop and you know that they are not going to stop because they haven't for the last five times you've tried to catch the Falmouth bus from Redruth. Bastards.

It was, frankly, a crap bus service between two towns in Cornwall, consisting of a handful of journeys each way at strange intervals. So odd were the timings and the various detours en route, it is tempting to believe that it was offered by First Western National purely as a means of moving their fleet around the county – the spasmodic nature of the service also meant that sometimes the bus simply failed to turn up at all.

Needless to say, my increasingly sarcastic and occasionally surrealistic correspondence with the bus company led to the occasional monopoly travel voucher being issued – a travel coupon that would never be used because, let's face it, turning up with a voucher that screams that you are an angry customer dissatisfied with the service is a bit like attending your Member of Parliament's constituency surgery with a prosthetic penis grafted to your forehead. The exchange is not likely to be productive.

Anyway, my Cornish bus stop woes pale into insignificance compared to the problems faced by passengers of a bus service – formerly managed by the local council – between Hanley and Bagnall in Staffordshire during the late 1970s. It highlights a case of what one commentator called a 'procedural illusion of effectiveness'. The bus, to cut a long story short, never ever stopped at one particular bus stop, even if there was a queue of 30 passengers waiting. After furious letters of complaint were published in the local newspaper, Councillor Arthur Cholerton replied that the buses didn't stop because if they did it would 'disrupt the timetable'.

Basket cases

In compiling a book of this ilk, there is naturally a danger of taking a lot of half-baked misinformation that gets passed around as Chinese whispers and re-presenting it as fact, so I am grateful to the Trades Union Congress (TUC), which published a report in 2006 called 'Health and Safety Myths, Looking at the Truth Behind the Headlines'. The purpose of the report seems to be to respond to some of the ludicrous stories highlighted by business organisations to moan about interference by the 'health and safety police' – the tabloid-coined phrase on the tip of the tongue of every fulminating little Englander.

One such story is that of the council that banned hanging

baskets on health and safety grounds, a story which the TUC classifies as a half-truth.

'This probably relates to Bury St Edmunds where the borough did briefly remove hanging baskets because of concerns that some lampposts were unstable', says the report. 'As soon as they had checked the lampposts, the hanging baskets were replaced.' With barely concealed joy, the report adds that, 'There are still hanging baskets in Bury St Edmunds.'

Like all half truths, however, this isn't the whole story either, because it is not only the Suffolk town of Bury St Edmunds where the quintessentially English love of gaudy blooms has fallen foul of common sense. A Somerset publican had his begonias condemned by council officials because they were hanging below the statutory 8 ft 2 in and people could bang their heads on them. The first thought that struck me was that they obviously breed them very tall in the pretty village of Norton Fitzwarren, but further research reveals that the 8 ft 2 in height – about 2.5 metres – is the potential clearance required for an officer of the law, complete with helmet, in full glorious bounding pursuit of a villain.

Meanwhile, parish councils in Staffordshire were ordered to stop using lampposts to hang baskets from because 'heavy watering' of the baskets could apparently flood the columns' electrics. They have either never seen rain in Staffordshire or their lampposts are made of something porous like cardboard. Either way, we should be told.

Staffordshire County Council, the source of the daft advice, also threw in the fear of baskets falling on pedestrians for good measure. The hapless council official charged with the task of writing to all the parish councils – the village hall committees that are playing with our lives so recklessly – holds the post of Intelligent Transport Systems Manager. Sometimes the satire just writes itself. Incidentally, as far as I have been able to ascertain, only once has a hanging basket fallen from a lamppost and injured a pedestrian, and that was because the lamppost itself was hit by a truck.

Fans of joined-up government will appreciate the next basket case to come under the purview of the world of flowers in the air. North Lanarkshire Council decided, like many forward thinking municipal authorities, that cheering up the streets with flower baskets was one of its responsibilities. But this cheery plan was doomed to failure. It would fail because, in order to work, it required the Holy Grail of Local Government procedure to occur – coordination between two separate departments.

The Leisure Services Department was charged with the responsibility to acquire a number of hanging baskets for the scheme to brighten up the streets of Motherwell, Coatbridge and Airdrie. But the department changed the specification to a larger and heavier basket without asking the Highways Department about the new design. As a result, a lamppost collapsed under the weight of the flowers. Motherwell,

Coatbridge and Airdrie were then deflowered and a detailed analysis of the structural integrity of 56,000 lampposts was undertaken. Welcome to the arcane world of North Lanarkshire Council, desperately trying to do the right thing, failing to look after the details and then saddled with an exercise so detailed it elevates tedium to a level equivalent to waiting for polypropylene to rot.

The lack of coordination has cost the council about £20,000.

Our final tale of basket-weaving bureaucracy brings us back to East Anglia, this time to Fakenham in Norfolk, where hanging baskets adorn many of the town's buildings, 21 of which are listed. Because of the listed status of those 21 buildings, special planning permission has to be given to fix metal brackets that hold up the baskets – but the consent was only given for three years because North Norfolk District Council wanted to 'protect the character of the town' and permission would have to be renewed at the end of that period.

When it came to that renewal, it took Janet Holdom, the founder of Fakenham in Bloom and volunteers at Fakenham Town Council, 25 hours to fill in 300 pages of forms to keep those 21 baskets attached to the buildings. It then cost £350 to advertise the planning applications in the local press. Every owner of the buildings concerned had to be informed that an application for planning consent was being made on their behalf, a photo had to be taken of each identical bracket and four forms had to accompany the application for each basket. Each of the four forms for each of the basket brackets then had to be copied four times and supplied with planning drawings and the photograph.

The North Norfolk District Council planning officer in charge of the application was said to be minded to make consent permanent this time.

You are not welcome around here

Hanging baskets notwithstanding, the world is a frightening place, doubly so in metropolitan areas. In fact, it's a rock-solid certainty in these troubled times that around almost any corner a new menace could lurk, skulking in the half shadows of some neon-lit urban walkway, where toddlers chew live ammunition and housing estates compete with one another – Britain in Bloom style – for which one can smell the most like tramp's piss. So, it was with some surprise that residents of Bristol City Council's public housing awoke one morning to find that the latest unspeakable threat to their safety, the agent of chaos in their midst, was none other than their humble doormat.

Residents of council-owned flats in the city were asked not to leave their doormats outside for health and safety reasons, apparently because they constituted a trip hazard. Failure to comply would result in confiscation and disposal of the lethal foot-wiping equipment.

Unable to furnish exact statistics on how many serious accidents or fatalities had occurred in the name of these unwelcome welcomes, Bristol City Council sensibly withdrew its demands for most of the city's 40,000 council tenants, choosing to crack down on the 2,000 weak and elderly occupants of its sheltered housing scheme instead.

According to delightfully imprecise information released by Bristol City Council under the Freedom of Information Act, the cost of the unwelcome initiative in terms of paper, printing, postage and manpower stands at 'not more than a few hundred pounds'.

Neither are yew

This was a lot cheaper than the last time that Bristol City Council found itself at the centre of unwanted attention, when it decided to uproot £5,000 worth of yew trees it had planted only the year before, after it carried out a risk assessment.

To be fair, the assessment was launched following 'concerns' – for which read 'blind hysteria' – from parents because the yew trees were planted between a café and a children's play area. Sometimes, you can't help noting that a little parental supervision, some wise words about nature and a touching confidence that your children aren't of the romantic suicidal poet persuasion, would be a lot safer for all concerned. Experts say although the leaves are mildly poisonous, it would take 'several handfuls' to induce vomiting.

A council spokesperson described the taste of yew leaves as 'foul' and said that it would take a 'very determined' person to actually harm themselves.

The subject of trees brings us to Norwich City Council, which has already made an appearance in these pages on the subject of time travel. Norwich felled 20 horse chestnut trees on health and safety grounds – lest a falling conker starts its life as a one-er by cracking open the skull of a hapless passing pedestrian.

Previous Norwich safety initiatives include banning window boxes at a block of flats and issuing directives on bouncy castles that alerted operators to the dangers of heavier children enthusiastically bouncing and catapulting their lighter peers into the air.

Kite fliers told to go fly a kite

The officers of Fylde Borough Council would regard 'a few hundred pounds' as quite cheap for a health and safety exercise: Fylde spent £15,000 on a risk assessment exercise on kite flying, after a woman walking a dog was tangled in the lines of a power kite at St Annes, near Blackpool. They also temporarily banned the flying of all kites – except traditional single string kites of the type favoured by children – from all beaches in the council's area. Not content with this, they then spent £18,000 on a beach safety plan so that all other shoreline activities, such as donkey rides, throwing Frisbees and the collection of driftwood, could be monitored and assessed.

With all the plans and assessments underway it would be reasonable to assume that it was safe to go on to the beaches in Fylde Borough, but what happens when the beaches come to you? After a particularly windy week of gales, Arthur Bulmer, who has a bungalow on the seafront at St Annes, found that roughly seven tons of sand had blown into his garden. His eminently sensible solution was to cart it back across the road in a succession of back-breaking wheelbarrow manoeuvres. Fylde Borough Council had other ideas, however. They told the pensioner that he could not put the sand back on the beach it came from as that would constitute fly-tipping and that he could be sent to prison for six months or fined up to £50,000. If that wasn't enough, they'd take his wheelbarrow away as well.

Disappointingly, Mr Bulmer had the whole lot eventually taken away by a waste management company.

A Fylde Borough Council spokesman maintained that 'nobody was threatened with prosecution', while adding, in the manner of someone itching to pass on a fascinating tit-bit of trivia, 'The sand is actually part of the Queen's Crown estate.'

From money to urn, via money to burn

If proof were needed that the world is going absolutely mad, East Hertfordshire Council can surely provide the evidence. You see, the council made their tea lady redundant and let staff help themselves to tea from a self-service urn instead of having it brought to their desk. Challenged by the new domestic arrangements, the staff then had a number of accidents including a scalded hand and, bizarrely, a broken wrist. Perhaps it was a very large cup of tea.

The council, who are obviously huge fans of irony, then spent £200 a day on health and safety consultants who advised staff, via a 17-page report, not to take trays of hot tea up and down the stairs. East Hertfordshire Council likes consultants, so much so that it spent £1 million on them over the course of the next three years.

Asked about the consultation, a spokesman for the Health and Safety Executive (HSE) seemed to distance themselves from what one councillor described as 'a storm in a teacup'. The spokesman told the *Hertfordshire Mercury* that it encouraged sensible health and safety, but 'this is not something the HSE has done in their own offices'.

Caution: do not walk into the warning sign

By the way, while we are on the subject of health and safety and the HSE, word is that some of the most accident-prone offices in the country are those of the Health and Safety Executive. Staff at the HSE are almost twice as likely to suffer a workplace accident as any other working people – where, for every 1,000 employees, there are an average of 21 injuries. At the HSE, that figure is 41.

Over a three-year period, there were over 500 Health and Safety Executive-related injured people. Of those, 96 were inspectors and 415 were at HSE offices around the UK. The accidents included a black eye caused by a falling toilet roll dispenser and, hilariously, an injury caused when someone walked into a warning sign. Your local HSE office is also quite a dangerous place to visit. Over the same three years, over 70 visitors were injured at Health and Safety Executive premises.

The blank cheque

'I've had several run-ins with Penwith District Council,' Terry informs us from his bullshit-proof bunker in deepest Cornwall. One amusing and, at the same time, utterly disturbing conversation with an officer of the council provoked the man behind the desk to say, 'You *are* just a number to us, Mr Sands.' Even without *The Prisoner*-esque quotes, Terry was already familiar with their customer care charter so, when on another occasion, the council sent him a blank cheque, he was bemused and confused, but not exactly surprised.

'It was the full works,' says Terry, 'watermarked, silver-foiled, signed, made out to me, but otherwise blank and ready for real numbers.'

Terry tells us, 'I'll admit that I was tempted to do the obvious, especially as they owed me money due to their prevailing incompetence. Honesty got the better of me, however, and I took it in to their offices. Rather than thank me for being an upright citizen, I got the worst end of their customer care charter again, when they virtually accused me of running a sophisticated fraud and counterfeiting operation from my damp flat, manufacturing cheques which I then – for in their eyes I was both unaccountably dense and incompetent – handed straight back to them.'

In the manner of the browbeaten and confused, Terry simply went home and quietly waited six weeks to be paid.

Not in my front yard

Just like the story above of the council officer with the some-what Orwellian view of his client base, many officials seem to believe that they are dealing with a troublesome record from a database rather than a living, breathing person. It is the mark of the truly officious that they treat their clients as impediments to their progress, but you would expect more from a politician, who are expected these days to have the human touch, surely? Not so in Derby, where the actions of householder Richard Butler undermined Chris Williamson, the leader of the city council so much, that he was forced to tell the local newspaper that, like some dreadful old paternalistic secondary school headmaster ticking off a pupil for making farting sounds during morning assembly, he was 'very disappointed' with his actions.

Derby City Council, you see, wants to build a £35 million ring road through Mr Butler's front garden and he is, understandably, rather upset about it. Refusing to voluntarily give up his marigolds and petunias to an ecological nightmare that would affect the heritage and environment of the city, he knew that it was only a matter of time before the council started to issue compulsory purchase orders in order to grab his garden. Eschewing the way of legendary road protestor, Swampy, Mr Butler did not chain himself to a bulldozer, dig a network of tunnels or take up residence in the canopy of a forest; his opening gambit, with fellow malcontent Trevor Lloyd-Davies, was to put up banners against the scheme.

The banners didn't work and, worse still, the council asked him and Mr Lloyd-Davies to take them down because, under the Town and Country Planning Act, they were regarded as advertisements. The two men refused to back down and were eventually taken to court by the council. Interestingly, there were dozens of other illegal, commercial banners hanging off pubs and the like and accusations of 'selective enforcement' were, unbelievable as it may seem, levelled at the council.

In the end, the forces railed against free-for-all banner anarchy won the case, but Mr Butler had hatched a cunning plan. In order to thwart the council, he began selling off plots of his lawn for £1 each, leaving Derby City Council with the onerous and lengthy task of tracking down all the owners of plots in Mr Butler's garden and serving compulsory purchase orders on all of them. Given that they live as far afield as Italy and China, this will take some time and delay the building of Derby City Council's inner ring road, even if it fails to stop it.

Going nowhere very slowly

Sometimes, though it may be hard to believe, a new road just does not get built at all, despite everybody agreeing it would be a terribly good idea. One such road was the A907, a project of Central Regional Council in Scotland, which became a victim of local government reorganisation when, in the mid-1990s, Central Region reverted to the patchwork of traditional counties it had been up until 1974.

Shortly before it was disbanded, Central Region Council started busying itself with arrangements that could not be followed through – in the manner of a deckchair attendant aboard the Titanic. The mark of a true bureaucracy is, after all, purely to satisfy its own goals for its own sake, rather than take account of any external circumstances. Before the light in the eye of Central Region was finally snuffed out, the council had just enough time to construct half a mile of road east of Stirling, on its way to Alloa. The road may have been on its way, but it never arrived, coming to a dead end after half a mile of cul-de-sac. Once the local authorities were re-shuffled, responsibility for the road project fell to two councils, Clackmannanshire and Stirling. For nearly ten years, this stretch of road remained completely unused and was known locally as the Road to Nowhere.

Refuse refuseniks

Mark Crane had just moved into his home on a brand new development in North Cornwall. After leaving his rubbish out for collection on the appropriate day, he was surprised to find it still there in the evening.

'A quick phone call to the local council revealed the problem,' Mark tells us. Apparently, the road had not yet been adopted and, as a result, the council was not prepared to risk their fragile and delicate bin lorries becoming damaged. According to Mark, he was then told to 'carry his rubbish up the road and leave it on the corner – on the crest of a substantial pile of rubbish from all the other houses on his street'. That's a nice bit of health and safety for you.

Certain that the council official was talking rubbish in every possible way, Mr Crane then tried to argue that other companies – among them Royal Mail, who do not have the words 'daredevil' or 'wild abandon' anywhere in their mission statement – had no such concerns about driving around those uncharted areas of the town so far unclaimed by the council. But the official was adamant, he wasn't going to play fast and loose with something as feral and potentially barbaric as an unadopted road.

The recycling collection, also run by the council, dutifully collected Mr Crane's recycling the very next day from the road less travelled outside his house. Nobody was harmed.

Walking away from Lambeth – how to not live there

If it appears that some councils are not at all bothered about those bits of their domain yet to be officially adopted, others won't leave you alone even if you live a long way outside their borders. Jamie recounts this tale of extreme municipal indifference.

'I lived in a tiny little flat in Clapham for five years and was subject to the extortionate council tax rates of the Borough of Lambeth,' he tells us. For the flat, which he describes as a 'handkerchief-sized abode', and the 'frankly awful services offered by Lambeth' he felt that paying nearly £100 a month in council tax seemed a 'tad pricey'.

In his defence, Jamie tells us that the general ambience of the area left a lot to be desired – physical and verbal assaults were common, while he also had the pleasure of watching passing locals discharge the contents of their bowels in his front garden.

Eventually he moved to Colliers Wood which, 'whilst not known for its hip, cool bars and witty haircuts, seemed pleasant enough'.

Now in the Borough of Merton, he was finally able to cut his Lambeth links. The tax was cheaper and his dwellings were larger, but what capped it off nicely was that the locals seemed to know how to use the bathroom.

'A few weeks after I'd settled in, I received a letter from Lambeth. To my gut-wrenching horror I was informed that not only did I owe them £800, but they'd instructed their bailiffs to retrieve monies. The reason was simple: I'd failed to pay my council tax. The fact I wasn't even living in Lambeth, and the money I 'owed' them was from the date of leaving to the present, seemed to be of absolutely no concern.

'Using all the relevant reference numbers, evidence of my moving, even a copy of the original letter I'd written to Lambeth informing them of my departure, I replied and quite reasonably thought no more of it. Oh, what a fool I was back then!

'A week later and then every other day, a red letter with Lambeth scrawled all over it dropped like a turd into my hallway demanding more and more sums of money. The bailiffs were coming. Prison was mentioned. In all honesty, I was getting scared. The constant threat that, at any given moment, my flat could be full of skinheads cheerfully lifting my electrical goods and furniture into a waiting van was making me extremely anxious.'

Jamie tried calling the bailiffs, but there was no reply. Then he tried calling Lambeth, but found that it made no difference. 'The fact that nearly everyone in Lambeth Council struggles with English wasn't very helpful. Neither was being randomly cut off, being put on hold for hours or that weird telephonic limbo, when the music and announcements stop and you hear half a second of an office full of people laughing, then five minutes of dead air. My heart was taking the toll, I could feel the veins on my neck boil with frustration – they were trying to kill me.

'The most vexing part was that I wasn't actually living in Lambeth – and they knew it. They were writing to me at my new address, an address they had because I had given it to them when I moved. When I explained this, in admittedly rather forceful terms after getting through to some department or other, they hung up on me. They still owe me for the door I put my foot through.

'I then reasoned that if they were sending me the same letter, albeit with ever-increasing amounts and more hysterical threats, there was no reason I shouldn't send them more vitriolic replies with the same basic information, at the same volume. For every one of theirs, they got one back. I included utility bills, parking permits, local shopping receipts even a photograph of me stood outside my house with the door open pointing at my hallway with "I live here" scrawled on it in permanent marker.

'This harassment went on for nearly six months, until one day, following a semi-genuine attempt to acquire an automatic weapon with the sole purpose of entering Lambeth HQ and randomly opening fire on their staff, I got through to a person with such ease and efficiency that I was forced to look at myself in a mirror to ensure it wasn't some sort of acid flashback. This person knew my name and everything; just as I began he stopped me.

'"This has been going on long enough, sir," he said. "Please be assured that no action of any kind will be taken against you. There has been an administration error. We apologise."

'I was quite literally speechless, my mind stumbling over

foul language, questions, demands for compensation, uncontrollable foreskin-ripping rage was replaced by Eastern mysticism. Ommm. Ommm.

'"Thank you, sir," I said creepily, "if you would be so kind, may I have that in writing?"

'"Of course, sir," my saviour replied, "it will be dispatched first class."'

Our hero didn't know whether to faint, vomit or cry.

'Thank you,' he said, as he let the phone gently down onto the cradle.

'In all honesty, following the delivery of my ironic absolution, this is the first time I've thought of this episode; I am quite sure that it took five years off my life and I am keen not to make it ten. Ommm Ommm.'

CHAPTER 4

The Commercial Breakdown

Tales of trains, spam and internal memos

You can telephone with a telephone; you cannot do anything else with it. And though this is one of the wildest joys of life, it falls by one degree from its full delirium when there is nobody to answer you.

***What's Wrong with the World*, G.K. Chesterton**

You are a curse to the civil service and you know it. If you think you know any better, try telephoning any part of it and listen. Those telltale little sighs you hear when they actually get around to picking up the phone to speak to you are not for nothing, and if you look at it from their point of view, it is easy to see why a life flying a desk for Her Majesty's Government is such a royal pain.

Many civil servants, it seems, are not only responsible for the intolerable burden of bureaucracy you find yourself under, but are actually victims of red tape themselves; memos, diktats, internal guidelines and best-practice manuals all handed down by their couldn't give a toss managers responding, in turn, to more of the same from their leaders and ultimately their leaders' leaders, all make for a life of drudgery under the neon tubes flickering at the exact frequency required for employee mind control. Then, to cap it all, the whole service is despised or ignored by its political masters and the wider world of the general public, who are egged on by the tabloids who harass and harangue it with every new variant of the European directive on the straightness of bananas story. And there you are, with your customer requirements, your service level expectations and your complete inability to fill in a form, along with your very British fear of authority and allergy to every item of mail bearing some kind of shield or seal, and you keep coming back for more. How dare you?

It is hardly surprising, then, that as they pick up the phone, messages gallop down the neurones to their tongue, 'Just leave us alone and don't come back.' But a last-minute thought about pension provision shunts the message into the nervous system's equivalent of a railway siding, where it manifests itself as an unconscious nervous tic four centimetres north of its original destination. And a little sigh.

So, it's a general rule that on the whole, the people who work for the government don't want you in their offices, and don't want you to phone either, not unless they feel the urgent need to oppress you in some way.

Not so in the commercial world, where they never want you to leave. Where they always want to keep in contact on any thin pretext and where the name, address and telephone numbers of thousands upon thousands of people like you represent untold potential riches for their shareholders. Once you are in a corporate database, it can be a real struggle to leave. Who hasn't grown tired of mobile phone operators, double-glazing suppliers and insurance sales people phoning up on the off-chance that you were considering purchasing one of these very things at that precise moment in time and not, for example, having a bath, eating dinner, watching TV or patiently kicking a door to door evangelical zealot to death in the hallway while screaming, 'Where is your God now?'

One bank even became so needy with requests for me to attend 'customer reviews', it bordered on stalking. Then, when all incoming telespam calls were stopped by resorting to the Telephone Preference Service, they started to email instead, pleading somewhat pathetically and with unreasonable desperation, that my family was missing out on great product news and valuable information.

For all the persistence, however, you'd think that there would be limits. Apparently not, even, as it turned out in one case, if you are dead.

Very little help

Claire, a good friend of mine, suffered the almost unimaginable grief of losing both parents in the space of eight months and losing them with vile haste, only being in her early twenties. Having carelessly lost both my parents already and remembering how officialdom intruded on the process, I am grateful to Claire for keeping tabs on the various impertinences of bereavement in the UK.

It is a human defence, in the face of grief, to keep busy – so some of the sombre formalities of death actually come as a welcome relief from churning over the same irreconcilable facts in your head over and over again. However, there's a difference between having something to occupy and distract you on the one hand, and fashioning a monomaniacal obsession on the other.

If there was a line to be drawn, I would suggest that it should be drawn some way before the notoriously complex Inheritance Tax form, which simply wants to take all of your attention, along with 40 per cent of your heirlooms. Recently confirmed as Britain's most difficult tax form by no less an authority than the National Audit Office, even the short four-page version of the Inheritance Tax return was the 10th hardest of all Revenue and Customs forms to fill out, with 74 boxes to complete and 38 pages of extra guidance notes. The full eight-page inheritance tax return has 149 boxes to complete and comes with a staggering additional 154 pages of guidance notes.

Put in a valuation mood by the Inheritance Tax form, Claire arranged probate valuations with local estate agents – none of whom turned out be lifelong members of the good taste and tactful club. Despite telling the agents that it was a probate valuation and that she was the executor of her father's estate, one estate agent insisted on quizzing her, 'Where is your father anyway?'

'In the crematorium,' was Claire's blank reply.

Another of the agents even turned his entrance into a study in slow comedy, as he had to delay the viewing of the property for a minute or so to allow his light-reactive prescription sunglasses to fade and clear.

Desperate to make some progress, Claire decided to turn to the tide of junk mail she was receiving, partly as a distraction, but partly because seeing her father's name on mail every morning was just compounding the loss. As a first step she resolved to stop the mailings of Tesco's Clubcard, the loyalty programme of Britain's largest retailer.

Tesco's advertising strapline may well be 'Every Little Helps', but Claire found they should perhaps modify it to 'Very Little Help'. Her first call to the phone number was answered with the offensively abrupt mantra of the pissed-off automaton: 'We can't help you, our systems are down.' When she explained the circumstances of her call and asked whether they could take down the details to cancel the mailings, she was told that she would have to put it in writing.

Let us be clear here; your Tesco Clubcard, in the grand scheme of things, is just a stupid supermarket loyalty card, another device for collecting data, keeping tabs on the fascinating world of your shopping and ensuring that you keep returning to the store. It is not a credit card, a national insurance number or a passport. Its value to the living is humble at best and to the dearly departed it has no value whatsoever: the ferry across the Styx does not give points; at the gates of heaven, the vouchers are invalid. It is a Tesco Clubcard which, despite its advertised properties of saving you one per cent off your shopping is ultimately merely another way of chiselling more money out of you and to hell with the consequences.

Unfortunately, that wasn't the end of it. Claire sent Tesco the Clubcard, a covering letter and – just to cover all the possible bases – a copy of the death certificate. A name, an address, the offending, unwanted Clubcard and a death certificate. Not good enough, apparently. When I caught up with her halfway through the unnecessary palaver, Claire was being harassed by answerphone messages to call Clubcard HQ, because the name and the card number didn't match. She was to call a non-geographic number and then take her place in the usual call centre queue to take the matter forward. Naturally, she declined.

Canning the spam

'How would you feel if somebody phoned you up, emailed or wrote to you to and implied that you were a gormless sap?' asks Mike, who is clearly quite angry. 'And what if, while they were insulting your intelligence, they asked you for money? You'd tell them what you thought, wouldn't you? But what if you couldn't?'

Now in full magnificent fulmination, Mike explains. 'I got a phone call from an advert. A monologue addressed to me, as a "specially selected" customer, which lasted for a minute, and offered me no chance to answer because there was nobody there. It was a recording urging me to call a £1.50 a minute phone number for seven minutes to claim my prize.

'I'm a grown-up. I know the score. You don't get anything

for nothing and, I expect, you get very little for a £10.50 phone call over and above a wad of Monopoly holiday vouchers. Or a hotel break where the cost of your unwanted off-peak room overlooking a cockroach and poo incinerator is more than covered by the ludicrous bill for your lunch.'

Railway network: 'nothing more than gravy train' shock

Britain's railway system is nowhere near the finest in the world, but at least it is a rich seam of cheap comedy. This 'cheap' humour costs just £5 billion per year to maintain – much less expensive than the NHS or the education system and for far more laughs. Looking at it from the perspective of a tax-paying, ripped-off customer, it's tempting to think that this is probably what the government means by value for money.

Among the more hilarious goings-on of the rail industry are thousands of passenger hours wasted by delays attributable to 'leaves on the line', the 'wrong kind of snow', 'heavy dew' and, in one case, a 'steep rise in atmospheric pressure'.

Welcome to the topsy-turvy world of the rail system. An upside-down universe of fun, apparently run on guesswork and flippancy. Connex, who used to run the troubled franchises to the south and south-east of London, ordered 3,000 uniforms for their staff without knowing, or bothering to enquire, what size any of their staff were. They then dispersed – the word distribution implies logistic know-how – the mixed set of uniforms willy-nilly across its network without even a forlorn attempt to make the best of the situation.

The same train operator ordered 55 new trains at a total cost of £200 million, waited three years, and then found out that they consumed too much power to run on their network. One mooted outcome was to run them at a lower power rating, leaving them slower than the trains they were replacing. Meanwhile, the company also admitted to tearing out seats on commuter trains as an experiment into passenger comfort and convenience. I'm sure that we all would have trouble imagining what the findings from the experiment could possibly have been.

At the turn of the millennium, the word Connex was roughly synonymous with the idea of an inefficient, dirty, overcrowded rail system – the network that was in place at the time. Things have improved marginally over the intervening years, but there are still stories from the trackside that can horrify and amuse at the same time.

Take, for example, the whole business of 'delay attribution', which employs about 300 people in the rail industry as a whole. It is essentially a matter of passing the buck for train delays between Network Rail, who own the tracks and signalling, and the train operating companies (TOCs) – who

... er ... operate the trains. The purpose of this exercise in timetable accountancy is to apply heavy fines to the company found at fault for each delay. There is a time limit to make things fun and, like a game of corporate spin the bottle, the blame and the fine rest with the last person to be pointed at. It is not recorded whether anyone has to take their clothes off, however. Naturally, with corporate ineptitude being in such abundant supply, there is a lot of healthy competition to not only look marginally less bungling but also to collect the handsome financial rewards on offer. In fact, the reason why delay attribution is so well staffed is that some operating companies make more money out of it than running the actual services.

Let the strain take the train

Aitch from Norwich supplies us with a fine example that shows why this internal market in blame attribution is not helpful in running the railway and, in fact, how it can just make everything more inconvenient for passengers.

'Don't talk to me about the train operator regulations,' he says, convincingly. 'It seems that they are fined for late trains and have to pay compensation if delayed more than an hour, but are fined even more if they actually have to cancel a train.'

Aitch has, it turns out, been inconvenienced by this rule on two occasions. Turning up at London Liverpool Street with 10 minutes to spare to catch the hourly service home to Norwich, he has watched as his service slips out of the station apparently 10 minutes early. But it wasn't so much 10 minutes early as 50 minutes late.

Says Aitch, 'The problem with this is, if the trains are hourly but running 50 minutes late, the sensible thing would be to cancel a train and effectively add another 10 minute delay, because then the trains would be leaving each station at the right time.

'But they'd be fined heavily for a cancellation, so they just carry on running 50 minutes late all day.

'So, people turn up on time for their train and find they've just missed one and then have to wait 50 minutes for the next one. Absolutely crazy.'

Dodgy fare

It seems that having a ticket is not enough to board a train any more. Two passengers travelling on a Virgin train from Edinburgh to Newcastle were approached for their tickets by a ticket collector. The pair dutifully presented them, but were taken aback when they were then asked to produce a receipt for them. The ticket collector even told them that they could have picked up the tickets from the street somewhere for all he knew and that if they were unable to show him a receipt or did not purchase another ticket, they would have to get off the train at the next stop.

Not wishing to cause a fuss, nor wishing to interrupt their journey for the principle, the pair gave in to this ludicrous demand and agreed to spend another £80, hoping to get it all sorted out later with someone less implacable at Virgin's customer services. They should have seen it coming really – and the clue is in the words 'customer services' – but imagine their surprise when they came up against another brick wall and were told that they could not be refunded for an unused ticket.

Eventually, under the watchful eye of Newcastle *Sunday Sun*'s consumer vigilante, Mr Justice, the pair were refunded; Virgin apologised and handed out some free tickets. Let's hope they sent them the receipt as well.

You need a password to retrieve your password

Ralph writes to us from London. 'I was gutted when my online auction account was hijacked by some sinister and shadowy underworld figure from the Chinese Mafia or, as was more likely the case, some script kiddie finding an easy electronic back door and helping himself to the proceeds.'

While seemingly unimportant in the scheme of things, the

consequences of account hijacking can be more than just frustrating and can even escalate to general identity theft: 'I was especially annoyed not least because I had always been very careful with online transactions, never coughed up my password in the wrong place, never visited the spoof sites and was generally – I thought – smart about how I used the internet.

'Taking all of that as read, I always thought that I would be able to keep one step ahead and keep my online stuff safe, so God knows what went wrong but, whatever it was, 40 dodgy videos were up for sale on my account in less time than it takes to say counterfeit DVDs. I, or rather the Mafiosa tweenie hackers using my name, were simultaneously on a bidding spree for more of the same and didn't mind how much it cost them because, frankly, it wasn't actually going to cost them a single penny.'

To stop the rot, Ralph tells us, the site helpfully reset the password. Unfortunately, they then slipped, with alarming ease, into becoming immediately unhelpful with a vengeance.

'Once they reset the password,', according to Ralph, 'this particular site falls back on a routine designed for people who have simply forgotten their passwords.'

Like many similar websites, the forgotten password routine is a secret shared knowledge system and, in order to tell you what the new random password is, it prompts you to enter those exotic little facts that theoretically only you and they know. Things like your homosexual great grandfather's maiden name, or the diameter, in centimetres, of your first pet's food bowl.

'The trouble is,' says Ralph, 'the identity thief had changed one of those secret questions so I had to resort to the website's help system to contact a human being to assist me in getting my account back.'

Help systems of this kind are often a bit patronising. Most of us can deal with user-friendly, but some of the advice is so obvious that it appears to be aimed not merely at a novice in the confusing world of the Internet, but someone so colossally inept, you wouldn't trust them with anything as complex as a two-inch pointed stick.

True to form, the help system was indeed extraordinarily patronising, just not that helpful. There are no phone numbers on the website anywhere and no email addresses either. Instead, when you require human assistance on this particular site, it presents you with a series of online multiple choice forms that you work through, which steadily filter your query through their various electronic corridors until you come to the final form where, it is promised, your enquiry can finally be sent to a help desk staffed by carbon-based life forms. So far, so good except, that when you need to contact someone about your account – you know, the one which you are no longer in control of because you no longer have the password – this final form asks you for your password.

All of this would be perfectly fine – if occasionally irritating – if when you finally found a loophole to email through, as Ralph eventually did on the fourth time of trying, somebody in customer support actually reads the email and answers the query made.

'They didn't. Three times I wrote to them with the same information, and three times the same email came back entirely missing the point. Admittedly there were variations – little cut and paste embellishments of individual personalities to attempt to convince you that a human is responding with more than a boilerplate email – but I was still left with the impression that my mail had not been read beyond the first line. Here's a tip folks, if you want to convince me that you are reading my email, it is very simple – try reading my email.'

Dotting the 'i's in fire!

'A few years ago,' writes Chris, clearly champing at the bit to get a classic tale of inter-departmental obstruction and feet dragging off his chest, 'I worked in an office in north London.

'One day, I happened to look out of my window and noticed a small plume of smoke curling from the litter bin in the smokers' courtyard.' Chris had noticed that a small fire had developed which also looked as though it could easily spread to nearby bushes.

Feeling that calling the fire brigade would be somewhat over-zealous, Chris rang the company's Facilities Management Department looking for a swift response that wouldn't cost the taxpayer an arm and a leg.

They asked him a series of questions about the nature of his request and then suggested calling the fire brigade.

'I explained that it wasn't really necessary,' says Chris, 'and that a member of facilities management could quite easily put it out. They informed me that in order to proceed with that course of action, I would need to raise an online work request. Before abruptly hanging up, they assured me that an engineer would be able to resolve the problem within 7–14 days.'

In the end, Chris writes, he put it out with a glass of water.

Exit strategy is good, but where is the exit?

But what if your fire needs a little more than a cup of water to extinguish it? Well, you would probably head for an emergency exit. Daniel writes in with a pithy example of a muddle caused by an all too brief official memo, sent out by email to all company employees. Its purpose was stated as thus: 'The following is our policy to follow if the facility is to be evacuated.' Short instructions followed on the exact no-nonsense procedures to be adopted. But, in the Where to Exit section of the memo, it all falls apart. 'The Emergency Evacuation Map shows the location of the emergency exits. You will find the Emergency Evacuation Map posted by each exit.'

CHAPTER 5

What?

*Tales of how gobbledegook, jargon and
spin get in the way of progress*

Political language is designed to make lies sound truthful and murder respectable, and to give an appearance of solidity to pure wind.

***Politics and the English Language*, George Orwell**

It is an odd affront to the teenagers of today that they are constantly bullied and patronised by those in positions of power for not having a good enough grasp of the English language. We hear how teenagers contort some words and invent others. We hear how they often use phrases that only a select group of their peers can understand. We hear also how they abbreviate everything and disregard formal grammar for the convenience of email and texting.

You can't help but think that this criticism is strange when the self-same powerful people who are pointing the finger at youth are often sophisticated manipulators of language for their own ends. They look, if the output of the official and legal world is anything to go by, to be doing precisely the same thing, albeit for different and dishonest reasons.

Where teenagers abbreviate for texting – a sensible response to the limited character count allowed by an SMS text – politicians, civil servants and captains of industry pepper their communications with abbreviations, acronyms and indecipherable contractions, as useful to communicating in English as hieroglyphics. Where formal grammar is stripped away, as with text, email and chat systems, it is about addressing your audience with an appropriate level of language for an informal medium. While youth talks to youth with neologisms and phraseology designed to exclude non-youth, those in positions of power also use specialist vocabulary and truth wrapped in dishonesty, in an effort to bamboozle the rest of us. The real difference in approach, however, is that our lords and masters are talking rubbish and systematically buggering the language from within.

One could easily fill an entire volume with comic double-talk, but I've tried to restrict this selection to not only the most absurd examples of tortured English, but also the ones where there is an attempt to introduce a layer of verbal bureaucracy between the writer and the reader.

How about this snippet of a press release from the West Midlands RIEP for introducing layers of verbal bureaucracy. It's something to do with ambulances and fire engines, apparently, but other than that it's anybody's guess. Nowhere in the release does it even mention exactly what RIEP stands for, apart from arrant twaddle, that is.

The press release wafts itself into the reader's consciousness with the following introduction. 'A Regional Capacity Building & Efficiency initiative in the West Midlands is the first of its kind in the country to receive joint funding,' it declares, seemingly unaware of how tedious this sounds. Emboldened by its opening statement, it drifts on: 'In a new development, the West Midlands RIEP recently approved a bid for £800,000 to drive forward a Business Process Re-engineering initiative.'

Business Process Re-engineering experts, eh? What will they deliver? Fortunately, that's a question that can only be answered by West Midlands RIEP: 'A small team of Business

Process Re-engineering experts will deliver a modular learning programme and populate a knowledge database for shared learning across the region.' Good grief.

Potty advice

We have all become used to the nagging nanny in our lives represented by the joint forces of public services, councils and government departments. Don't eat that, stop drinking, stop smoking, get more exercise, keep breastfeeding, it's all for your own good, you know. One recent case even saw a government department spending nearly a quarter of a million pounds on a leaflet highlighting the wild danger of wearing carpet slippers. Well, now they would like to tell you how to go to the toilet.

In 2006, a Tayside National Health Service Trust did just that when it issued a leaflet of tips for taking a crap.

Good Defecation Dynamics, for that is the name of the NHS advice, is a four-page leaflet that helpfully explains, with diagrams, to 'keep your mouth open as you bulge and widen' and 'do not forget to breathe'.

Money talks

Financial advisers and companies are often accused of

peddling gobbledegook and survey after survey of us, the British public, only confirms what we all know is so: virtually nobody has the faintest idea what is meant by the barrage of acronyms and plain vanilla initials on show in the average terms and conditions for a credit card.

Still, perhaps it's not surprising that the language of the financial services sector are so opaque and alienating when you consider that many of the parameters of pension, savings and investment schemes are, in effect, drawn up by the financial services industry's mother ship, the Treasury. Generally dreamed up and written for the benefit of its annual grand day out, the Budget – the regulations for which run to roughly 1,000 pages per year – esoteric mumblings of financial regulation prove time and time again that money itself has become the concrete manifestation of red tape, in that it is no longer necessary to produce something with it, just move it around for its own sake. Nothing is produced as a result of all this effort, except the braying of well-heeled and young, perfectly moisturised stockbrokers in a city bistro. Once again, the process has become the product, and the means to an end is the end in itself.

Moving all of this money around for whatever end naturally requires a lot of rules and regulations – a cursory glance at one of the Treasury's chief accounting instruments, the tax return, will tell you just how complex accountancy has become over the years – but the tax return itself is a model of concise clarity compared with some of the regulations it partially obscures from us.

As an example of how something gets twisted into an unintelligible mush, take these paragraphs from the 2000 Finance Act on the subject of the Climate Change Levy. If, like me, you find your eyes swivelling in and the furniture becomes blurry when you read the following passage, make sure you are sitting down for sub-paragraph (7)(c) or have a large glass of neat gin close at hand.

'7. Where the end of the balancing period is by virtue of sub-paragraph (2)(c) (averaging period ends after 2 years) the end of an averaging period, the supplier is liable to account to the Commissioners for an amount equal to the amount that would be payable by way of levy on a taxable supply that –

(a) is made at the end of the balancing period,

(b) is a supply of a quantity of electricity equal to the difference between the two totals, and

(c) is treated as a reduced-rate supply to the extent (if any) that the exempt renewable supplies made by the supplier in the averaging period would have been reduced-rate supplies if they had not been made on the basis that they were exempt.'

Now there's a paragraph that'll put hairs on your chest.

The department that can hardly contain itself

In a previous life, I ran a satire website called The Department of Social Scrutiny where, I was often heard to moan, the job of satirising a government department was made all the more difficult by its relentless determination to satirise itself.

On one of that site's spoof identity card registration forms, I cracked a gag about official definitions. 'Please estimate the number of rooms in your home' ran a request, with a helpful definition below, 'By "room" we mean a polyhedral space bounded by four walls, a floor and a ceiling. A cupboard counts as two rooms.'

But the Department of Health went one better and out-satirised the satire. Keen to wipe any element of doubt about exactly what constitutes a 'container' – the Department won themselves a Plain English Campaign, Golden Bull award with this ludicrous definition:

'"Container", in relation to an investigational medicinal product, means the bottle, jar, box, packet or other receptacle which contains or is to contain it, not being a capsule, cachet or other article in which the product is or is to be administered, and where any such receptacle is or is to be contained in another such receptacle, includes the former but does not include the latter receptacle.'

Almost as good as the celebrated definition of 'bed' made in a Welsh Office document in the early 1990s: '... a device or arrangement that may be used to permit a patient to lie down when the need to do so is a consequence of the patient's condition rather than a need for active intervention such as examination, diagnostic investigation, manipulative treatment, obstetric delivery or transport.'

You might have hoped that a definition of a prosaic household object like a bed that runs to 46 words would clear up all confusion on the matter, but you would be wrong. The definition resurfaced in a document 10 years later – slightly rewritten – in the Republic of Ireland's Ministry for Health and Children. A journalist's freedom of information request regarding a controversy over whether the Republic's government could possibly be fluffing the figures for the number of new hospital beds it was providing by counting new trolleys as well, revealed that what at first appears to be the definitive definition of 'bed' is hopelessly flabby and indistinct.

Grounded in pedagogy ...

Out of context, it has to be admitted, 'grounded in pedagogy' does sound like a particularly grubby criminal offence. Unusually, however, putting it in context – that of working with young people – only serves to make it sound even less wholesome. This phrase was unearthed in one corner of academia where clear communication is apparently no longer required, if this bite-sized, yet still indigestible morsel from the Higher Education Funding Council for England (HEFCE) is anything to go by.

In the HEFCE's Centres of Excellence in Teaching and Learning (CETL) programmes, the following paragraph describing the 'Embedding, Enhancing and Integrating Employability' course module was found.

'E3I's holistic approach advocates embedding and integrating a coherent range of employability features in programmes, benefiting all students, developing attributes needed for success in their chosen paths and lifelong development, and supporting widening access to employment. Our models and examples (policies, strategies and practices) will be adaptable to other institutions. Ongoing evaluation will contribute to employability research. Our holistic approach and our links into national and international HE communities will enable E3I to have a key sector co-ordination and dissemination role. Our articulation of employability and the curriculum features supporting it, grounded in pedagogy, research and our own evaluated practice, puts E3I at the cutting edge of practice.'

Given that 'Embedding, Enhancing and Integrating Employability' attracts HEFCE capital funding of £2 million and an annual grant of £500,000, it is indeed surprising that they couldn't afford either a decent copy editor for the tortured prose or some kind of violent punishment for the writer.

Another CETL document – this time at Manchester Metropolitan University, manages to tie itself up in knots in magnificent fashion.

Under a paragraph helpfully titled 'Affordances from taking part in the e-benchmarking exercise', we learn that 'The exercise has revealed opportunities for enhancing the uptake and development of e-learning by ensuring that local implementation is synergistically supported by close interaction with central units.

'These opportunities have led to a targeted Pathfinder Programme for Institutional Change, based on founding a local Leadership Change Academy.'

With material like that coming from faculty, it's no wonder that the student body pick up the habit of talking rubbish. At Oxford University, the Student Union wanted to get better access to city councillors and charged the union president and vice-president with the task of drawing up a document to push the case.

The seven pages of copy, designed to sway the council to their arguments that students should have non-voting positions on some committees, contained such esoteric sub-headings as Concept Premises and Process Determination and Actualisation.

However, these little sparkling jewels of gobbledygook paled into insignificance next to the following paragraph of twaddle.

'The formalisation of student participation in Full Council would facilitate a constructive symbiosis between City and student. Only through the institutionalisation of student representation on Council will Oxford's student sabbaticals be uniformly informed of and integrated into Council activities.'

A councillor was moved to comment, 'In places it was more unintelligible than even our officials can produce. It quite cheered them up.'

The council was clearly impressed; the Union increased the numbers of students on its committees.

Wooden English

On to the European Commission – frequently criticised for doublespeak of its own, it goes one further in this introduction to the European Union Forestry Strategy, 'The Commission Communication on the implementation of the EU [European Union] Forestry Strategy responds to the request of the Council to report on the implementation of the Strategy ...' So, in a metric nutshell, 'this report answers the call for this report'. You don't say.

Think tanks – those strange autonomous bodies that manage to pass off opinions as fact – are a particularly rich resource when it comes to gobbledegook. Perhaps it is because they are usually set up on the boundaries of two disciplines – business and politics or, economics and the voluntary sector, for example – and must work hard to fill the chasm between the sectors with a mutually agreed language, a voluminous say-nothing void that fills up reports and papers with a lexicon of nonsense, without promoting the urgent need to actually do anything.

One such body is the Overseas Development Institute (ODI) which, according to their website, is 'Britain's leading independent think tank on international development and humanitarian issues'. Notwithstanding their benign and honourable intentions, the ODI seeks not to hide its bright light under a bushel so much as to secrete it in a sealed lead box. Its reports can use spectacularly opaque language – language that appears to be more interested in communicating the rigorous academic process of compiling the paper than the message contained somewhere within. In one report – on God knows what, for I pride myself in being academically shallow – a paragraph entitled, 'Lessons learned which might inform debate on livelihood protection-promotion synergies', delivers the following mystifying message.

'We have to start with a fundamental difference: we have argued in the body of this paper that there are potential synergies between livelihood protection and promotion, and that it may be important to sequence interventions. But in the humanitarian discourse, the notion of a continuum from relief to rehabilitation to development has proven largely elusive in practice.'

But there's yet more baloney to come and most of it comes from politicians, or is inspired by political motives. It proves once more that there is now usually no requirement for lying when the verbal dexterity of official spokespeople is enough to conceal the tiny – and sometimes devastating – kernel of truth in what you say.

However, followers of Britain's one-time Deputy Prime Minister John Prescott are more relaxed, as they are merely tasked with finding the kernel of meaning in such gems as:

'I personally have always had that to my mind, and in particular for the consequences of fire service. I visited my fire stations. They posed the question of what is the work of the firefighter, and that precisely what we have to dress ourselves to this. That should be the front of every one of us. It's certainly to the front in my intentions, and I intend to see we can achieve it.'

Tough on crime, tough on the definition of crime

As already noted, we are often regaled in the popular media with tales of how many of the young of the nation are functionally illiterate and uncommunicative slobs talking among themselves in impenetrable and obtuse language about stuff of no interest to wider society. If that tabloid crite-rion for defining 'youth' strikes a chord with you, you should perhaps take a look at the literature of the Birmingham Community Safety Partnership and be convinced that they were the incoherent ramblings of an under achieving gang of tweenies.

Unlike your average group of estranged youth however, the Birmingham Community Safety Partnership are not a flick-knife wielding gang of rat-children in hoodies from a god-forsaken estate and don't really have any excuse for talking bollocks as they are all presumably over the age of majority. What they have in common, perhaps, is a need to communi-cate in code to disguise certain unpalatable truths. With the hoodies, it's bravado and big talk, with the Partnership possibly it is, as one commentator noted, a case of, if no one understands what you are promising, nobody can criticise you for not delivering. Perhaps that's why the Partnership decided in its Crime and Disorder Reduction Strategy docu-ment that it would start with a definition of crime:

'Its causation reflects a complex interaction of structural risk factors that result in the emergence of crime and disorder as problematic to specific neighbourhoods and places, both in the immediate and medium to longer term contexts. The Partnership believes the majority of crime to be the inter-active product of offenders engaging with victims (or targets) at locations that lack effective guardianship and are thus perceived as being conducive to crime.'

Fantastic stuff, I think you'll agree.

A play on words

It should be child's play to define but, according to St Helen's Council in Lancashire, 'The freely chosen and personally directed enactment of a group of non-goal-orientated behaviours which become progressively more complex with experiences and which in themselves facilitate the development of an equivalent range of tools without which species cannot continue' nails down 'children's play' in a satisfactory fashion.

Which, in turn, reminds me of this description of go-karting for excluded kids, dreamed up, in what can only be some kind of severe mental aberration – a kind of peculiar disorder that renders the victim unable to write anything without first describing it at molecular level. According to someone at Luton Borough Council, the go-karting programme is, 'a multi-agency project catering for holistic diversionary provision to young people for positive action linked to the community safety strategy and the pupil referral unit'.

Working title

Meanwhile, how long is your job title? They can be almost as long as your job description if this position advertised by a branch of Lancashire County Council's Library Service in Preston is anything to go by. The actually rather dull sounding post of 'temporary part-time Libraries North-West Inter-library Loan Business Unit administration assistant' was advertised for in 2005.

While 'temporary part-time Libraries North-West Inter-library Loan Business Unit administration assistant' may be the longest job title on offer, others compete with it if only in terms of their silliness. I was unable to find the exact council responsible for advertising for an 'education centre nourishment production assistant', but I do hope it manages to find a new school dinner lady sometime soon. Meanwhile, in a national poll organised by the jobs2view.co.uk website, that description of a dinner lady was narrowly ahead of 'waste removal engineer' or bin man, but rightly pipped to the top spot by the title of 'vision clearance executive' for window cleaner.

This would be all old news to you if, like me, you have ever had a job title promotion designed to make you feel better about your responsibilities without any attendant pay rise. I once worked in a small creative enterprise as an administrative assistant and had my ego promoted to assistant administrator. No extra pay was wasted in the simple rearrangement of adjective and noun.

While these are all just silly ways of playing with names for perfectly sensible jobs – and designed for gratuitous ego inflation to offset a wage demand, it's astounding to find that there are daft job titles to describe what are plainly daft jobs, but for really quite attractive financial packages.

Aberdeenshire Council appears to lead the way, by employing two nursery rhyme promoters and, bafflingly, a trampoline officer. If you're seeking an explanation on what the officer is responsible for, turn to the council's website, where you'll find this helpful explanation of the work of the council's Head of Bouncing. Apparently, '[he] organises safety workshops in schools for garden trampolines. He also does coaching for various groups and advises generally on trampoline matters.'

One can't help but wonder where the arc of his career will lead him. Perhaps he'll end up as the Trampolining Ambassador to the United Nations one day.

There is much to be appreciated in proper and precise legal drafting of important pieces of legislation, standing orders, statutory instruments and other finely woven examples of legal flummery, especially where no doubt should be left as to their meaning. But it's quite something else when the man in charge of the bins at the local council goes wafting off on the hereto-therefore-afters. The following baffling correspondence from

Northumberland County Council to Councillor W.G. Weeks of Berwick upon Tweed Borough Council was released into the public domain. Apparently it's part of a letter addressing concerns raised by Councillor Weeks about the management of designated skips at the council tip. 'Removal of an employee of the waste takes that waste out with the definition of "household waste" and into waste termed "non-household waste".' If that leaves you utterly flummoxed you'll probably agree that, like many of our councils of imperfection, it does indeed appear to be full of rubbish.

War on words

Let me just finish this chapter on a downbeat note. I'll risk bumming out your happy humour book by making an observation about a chilling use of language intended to damp down a potentially damaging controversy.

The use of extreme euphemism to disguise unpalatable facts is well established enough in these violent yet media-savvy times. We are already familiar with friendly fire, collateral damage, surgical strike and the most horrific of all, ethnic cleansing. The soft touch of brutality is quite sickening, but it's nothing compared to this final example of war speak.

An official investigation into the case of two detainees beaten to death at a US base in Afghanistan concluded that they died by the 'repetitive administration of legitimate force'. It's clear in these circumstances that weasel words can help a speaker wriggle out of just about anything. In fact, 'repetitive administration of legitimate force' sounds almost humdrum and tedious, like the kind of thing a civil servant would do to sharpen a pencil. All the words have, in effect, been disassociated from their brutal reality – in keeping with their military objectives, the administrative wing of the US Army have defused a bomb.

CHAPTER 6

The Ministry Position

*Tales of how government departments
tangle themselves in red tape*

Seemingly from the dawn of man all nations have had governments; and all nations have been ashamed of them.

***What's Wrong With The World*, G.K. Chesterton**

Bureaucracy, the rule of no one, has become the modern form of despotism.
Mary McCarthy

We have arrived at our last chapter – the one concerned with the red tape recordings of government and the civil service and, in a sense, we have come home. Home, in that the rest of this work acts as an arrow pointing to the back of the book, as it neatly passes the buck ever upwards and toward the centre of things revealed here.

After all, the first mental picture that the phrase red tape conjures up is often that of the civil servant: a man in a pinstriped suit with a meticulously groomed moustache; a weasel-faced, pin-prick of a personality, slavering away at the prospect of ruining your day with obstruction and delay. Multiply that by half a million – the total number of employees in the civil service – and that is one very large office full of people engaged in aimless tinkering with the lives of all the hapless citizens in their thrall.

It is hard to avoid the thought that, no matter what admirable personal qualities the public official may possess, how exotic their tastes in cuisine, how intrepid and death-defying their last holiday was, even if raw animal magnetism percolates through their very soul, their grey vocation will puncture all excitement in its path. It seems as if the civil servant as a species is just not that popular. Indeed, the research phase of this book – when stories and anecdotes about the effect of bureaucracy on everyday life were canvassed – flushed out a whole slew of stories that seemed to complain about the very existence of the civil service itself. The most vitriolic responses came – mostly, it appears, from fundamentalist free marketeers who froth so magnificently about the deleterious effect of rules and regulations on business they seem to be one step away from stuffing waifs and strays up their chimneys.

However, while all that may be so, it is difficult to avoid taking the view that pen-pushing for the authorities is twice as thankless a task as filling in the forms in the first place. What is more, the officials are not immune and, as we will see, often have more than one pending tray full of oppressive bureaucracy to deal with themselves. It is just that we never see beyond the awkward little Hitler stereotype, to see the root cause of all our troubles. Because, no matter how efficient a country is at operating, someone has to clean the toilets, someone has to sweep the floors, someone has to make decisions and someone has to do the paperwork, therefore some kind of civil service is necessary. Fortunately, the odd jobsworth aside, the majority of civil servants are just that, public servants who have old-fashioned ideas about providing services for the public good and take their responsibilities to the rest of us seriously.

What none of us wants is a kind of uncivil service, but

unfortunately, as the following tales reveal, we already have a hardcore of a new type of service, one that is the culmination of all the previous chapters of this book. It has jobsworths aplenty, it has at its heart a slightly authoritarian, letter of the law concern for your wellbeing, and it is reinforced by gobbledegook, helpfully introduced by commercial institutions whose priority is not the business of delivering service, so much as being at the service of those who deliver their business.

Black tape

Oliver Wendell Holmes, the American author and physician, once wrote that, 'Insanity is often the logic of an accurate mind overtaxed.' How, it could be wondered, would that apply to those that tax us themselves, because it would seem that the powers that be at Her Majesty's Revenue and Customs (HMRC) have finally succumbed to a wild madness of their own. Perhaps it's the stress of marshalling the country's least popular bureaucrats around, but HMRC managers now appear to have listened to the voices in their heads and self-medicated with chainsaw lobotomies.

News comes our way that the national insurance office at Longbenton in Northumberland has been swooped upon by logistics consultants – for which read time and motion men – as part of a package to roll out their new and fundamentally anti-human 'Lean' programme: a campaign to clear clutter from desks and ban all personal items.

A spokesperson for the Public and Commercial Services Union (PCS) even told *The Times*, 'We had a situation in some offices in Scotland where staff were asked, "Is that banana on your desk active or inactive?", meaning were they going to eat it? If not, it had to be cleared away.'

Misplaced inactive bananas aside, as part of Lean everything has its place and, in order to enforce this principle, HMRC workers – apparently known affectionately as 'units' to their management – were given rolls of black tape to mark out where pens, pencils and keyboards go as well as to show the units where to place their phones.

(As an aside, having recently talked to one less than helpful member of staff at the HMRC on the telephone, I can definitely help with suggestions for finding a convenient place for their handset.)

Once they have organised their desks, the android HMRC units are given targets to attain, targets which rise with each regular team meeting they attend. According to sources within the HMRC, that regular meeting can be as regular as every hour on a bad day.

All of this was apparently the stunted brainchild of Unipart, consultants employed by Revenue and Customs to apply a revered philosophy of business that is known within the company as The Unipart Way. In common with most management consultants who attach a mystic brand value to a load of old codswallop scrawled on a Nobo pad, Unipart and HMRC have come over all mystical about the invoice value of the black tape and refuse to say how much this particular exercise has cost; however, the price tag for the Lean programme nationally is, according to the PCS, £7.4 million.

But hold on a minute, is that really Unipart? For readers that don't remember – and there's probably a good few that have tried hard to forget – Unipart was the state-owned automotive parts supermarket of British Leyland. Yes, British Leyland, the 1970s nationalised car manufacturer, the butt of three-quarters of the decade's non-racist jokes and arguably the UK's most shining example of a complete and utter business failure. It is a testament to the power of Unipart's marketing that anything formerly attached to British Leyland can become a brand for efficiency in business. You also can't help but feel that Unipart's transformation from supplier of air filters for the Austin Allegro to corporate desk tidiers for the tax office is rather a neat metaphor for what has happened to Britain over the last 30 years.

Turning IT to MT, misinformation technology

The Lean programme demonstrates a larger trend in public bureaucracy – time after time, projects like it are outsourced to business management and IT consultancies when common sense dictates, surely, that in such large organisations the expertise should be on hand. However, many consultants are merely employees who have been made redundant in the name of cost-cutting and then rehired at a considerable multiple of their former civil service income. HMRC, for example, spends £130,000 a day on approximately 200 consultants – an average of £650 a day each – because of an internal skills shortage. Those consultants may be working side by side with HMRC staff paid around £120 a day.

This all strikes me as the worst of all worlds. If having a civil service is good for one thing, it is good for attracting sharp minds to come and work on behalf of the public at non-extravagant rates, in exchange for job security and a career ladder. There is really no excuse for having hundreds of thousands of employees and still having a skills shortage. It's not as if those skills shortages are in particularly exotic or arcane areas of expertise either. Nearly 60 per cent of all consultants used by government are IT specialists. However, if there is truly such a dearth of programmers, system designers and developers on the civil service payroll, maybe it would go halfway to explaining why government IT projects are so often plagued by massive cost overruns, huge technical difficulties and, more often than not, last-minute cancellation.

The state's record with large information technology projects amounts to a magnificent catalogue of failure. That is the cold truth of the matter, but let me furnish you with some examples, some notorious, infamous even, and a few that may have escaped your attention.

The cost of justice scales new heights

A project originally launched over 15 years ago to standardise the IT systems of 370 Magistrates' Courts in England and Wales is still a long way from being completed.

The original specification goes back to January 1992 when the Home Office appointed Price Waterhouse to develop an IT system for the courts. However, by August of the same year, a shuffle of Whitehall's responsibilities had the project moved and it embarked on its long and fruitless association with the Lord Chancellor's Department. The Department immediately cancelled the contract, claiming that the contractor's work was 'sub-standard', and then, being of a legal persuasion, initiated proceedings against Price Waterhouse for £5 million in payments made.

In 1994, the Department had another stab with MASS – which stands for Magistrates' Court Standard System, even though it clearly doesn't. (Acronym accuracy was far less important in the 1990s; these days a committee would be charged with coming up with a dynamic sounding name and then making it fit as best they could, employing consultants who would simply make up a new word in order to keep up appearances.) By late 1996, the software had been written – though not tested – and things seemed to be progressing well until an independent review showed that the 'Department's strategy for delivery of the project was flawed'. The Department paid its MASS contractors some £6.8 million and terminated the contracts.

That same year saw the start of Libra, a new IT system for Magistrates' Courts that had some far-sighted features. So far-sighted, in fact, that the whole system is still being installed. The choice of Libra as a name is interesting. Presumably it was to refer to the symbolic scales – Libra being the Latin word for balance – held by the famous statue of Justice that is perched atop the Central Criminal Court in the Old Bailey in London, but we should also consider the alternatives. As we shall see, it might just mean pounds sterling as in the Roman system of coinage, LSD or *librae, solidi, denarii.* The £ symbol itself, fact fans, is derived from a form of the letter 'L'. Finally, we shouldn't discount the possibility that there is an astrological connection: the star sign Libra is also said to rule excretion.

In 1998, after one of the most apathetic tendering processes imaginable, the Libra project contract was awarded to ICL, the only contractor at all interested in doing it, as by the final hurdle, theirs was the only bid.

ICL originally said that they would do the contract for

£146 million in July 1998. By October 1998, having won the bid, they increased their bid to £184 million, because they appear to have got their costs and revenues wrong. After some negotiations, the Department duly rolled over and signed up to the new price.

A year later, in October 1999, ICL were back to renegotiate their contract – this time up to £319 million. In July 2002, after more panic attacks in the ICL boardroom, a new management team at the firm and some failures to meet delivery dates, the company – now called Fujitsu Services – withdrew from the software side of the deal and another contractor was found.

By 2006, the total cost of the project had risen to £442 million, with an extra £52 million being spent on software and £60 million on enhancements.

So after 15 years of planning and false starts, 10 years of Libra and hundreds of millions of pounds excreted into the porcelain bowl of justice, how many magistrates' courts were running the system? At the start of 2007, out of the 42 areas in the English and Welsh court system, three now have Libra and of the 370 magistrates' courts a grand total of 16 were connected up to Libra. But that's OK because another seven were coming online shortly. Whoopee-do.

IT's a complete shambles

It's not as though Libra is the only scheme that's gone horribly wrong either. Large government IT projects have a habit of collapsing under their own weight quite regularly. In 2001, the Home Office's snappily titled National Probation Service Information System Strategy – NPSISS – proved as unwieldy as its name and suffered cost overruns of 70 per cent according to the National Audit Office.

In 1999, the Ministry of Defence (MOD) was criticised – again by the National Audit Office – for frittering away £30 million on two bespoke systems, which were abandoned because they did not work properly. One of the systems was figuratively taken out, blindfolded and shot when it exceeded its total budget by 217 per cent in one year. An MOD spokesperson inevitably said that it had learnt its lesson from the projects which is why it is strange to note that the latest defence project, the Orwellian-sounding – no, strike that – the Orwellian project known as Skynet 5, is over budget by £2.6 billion.

Meanwhile, is it third time lucky for the increasingly desperate Child Support Agency (CSA), now on computer system version 3? Hardly: run by the Department for Work and Pensions (DWP), the CSA consumed £539 million over-hauling business and computer systems between 2000 and 2006, and £91 million on external advisers, only to scrap the lot by phasing out the entire agency. At one point, staff were so frustrated by the £456 million software on offer, they whipped out their pocket calculators to work out what people owed. In 2006 it emerged that, of every pound collected from absent parents by the agency, 70 pence went on administration.

Speaking in July 2007 as the Public Accounts Committee published its report into the beleaguered agency, committee chairman Edward Leigh observed that, 'The Department for Work and Pensions never really knew what it was doing in dealing with the contractors EDS and the system was a turkey from day one ... Three years after [the IT system] was introduced, it still had 500 defects and staff confidence has been seriously damaged.'

In an official report on the CSA, the Committee noted that there was little in-house IT expertise at the DWP and this meant it was not able to challenge the contractors or put right the numerous technical defects.

It's easy to look at the frankly gargantuan figures involved in IT systems procurement and to concentrate purely on the money squandered on this scheme or that, but dysfunctional IT has a much greater cost when it gets in the way of work being done. In the case of the Child Support Agency, one in four applications received since 2003 has still not been dealt with and, since the start of the CSA, there are £3.5 billion in uncollected payments. In 2005, the DWP's own research, alongside a government investigation into problems with the CSA, found that difficult cases were sometimes deleted on purpose by disillusioned staff. As an epidemic of low morale took hold, fuelled by an ever-lengthening backlog of cases, some staff even admitted to entering incorrect details into the system on purpose in order to move cases along. Some others worked out strategies to avoid awkward phone conversations with frustrated clients. None of this bears the hallmarks of an efficient, professional service and all of it only serves to make the difficult business of parents breaking up more fraught and vexatious for all concerned. After a difficult 13 years in the world, the teenaged Child Support Agency was finally axed in 2007.

It is a particular feature of government IT projects like those behind the CSA's woes, that when mistakes are made, they are never made just once. In the case of the Passport Agency, the same IT mistakes were made three times – once in 1992, then again in 1999 and 2006. In 1999, many holidaymakers missed their flights, still waiting for their passports because 500,000 were issued late. The queues formed at Passport Agency offices were so substantial and the weather so inclement that the Agency bought £16,000 worth of umbrellas to keep the queues dry. Then, in 2006, online passport applications, rolled out by the newly rechristened Identity and Passport Service (IPS), were started and promptly shelved again after yet more IT problems.

In 2007, the Department for Work and Pensions (DWP) sent out nearly 12 million letters to pensioners detailing what their pension payments would be over the next year. Trouble was they sent 26,000 of those letters – which contained bank account details, NI numbers and names and addresses – to the wrong people, thereby creating massive potential for rampant identity theft.

So what is my point, exactly? Well, the government wants to tie the databases of the latter two departments, IPS and DWP, together with that of a third, the Immigration and Nationality Directorate (IND). They want to tie them all together in order to create the new National Identity Register, the mother ship of all other government IT projects and just about the most unfeasible idea since someone tried to staple jelly to a moving cat.

Examine the evidence. Only 30 per cent of government IT projects succeed. The Department for Work and Pensions cannot post a letter. The Immigration and Passport Service have never been in possession of a decent, fully functional IT system. The Home Office and Department for Constitutional Affairs have, between them, presided over an IT project (MASS/Libra) that has not yet even been partially deployed after 15 years. Meanwhile, it is only early days for the NHS National Programme for IT (NPfIT) and it has already started to come apart with reports of critical components of the scheme being up to two years behind schedule.

All of these are big projects, but apart from the gargantuan NPfIT, they pale into insignificance next to the ID Register, which aims to catalogue, hold biometric samples and photographs of every single one of us – that's 60 million people – who live in the UK. In total, the ID Register will hold 50 pieces of identifying information about every one of us, including our fingerprints and what is referred to in the 2006 Identity Cards Act as 'other biometric information'. Quite apart from the sheer scale of the IT itself, the collection, input and storage of three billion pieces of data is a Herculean task. But it isn't just an enormous IT project; it is an enormous information and data collection project, a compulsory electronic Domesday Book that catalogues every single human life in the UK.

Add to that the fact that the information – which you are responsible for legally, but are not allowed to update – will be entirely in the control of a string of people you are not competent to judge the character and motives of, because that string of people is in the future. Your entry on a National Identity Register becomes your identity in the future, where that identity is, in effect your ticket to ride, your entitlement to be a citizen, your whole life and proof of who you are.

I can only imagine the possibilities for bureaucracy and the potential for abuse – maybe not tomorrow or today, but what about in 10, 20, 30 years time? A single mistake in the wrong place might rebound across the bureaucratic landscape, affecting everything from your tax code to your driving licence and dentist appointments. In the past, the frustration of dealing with anything where more than one government department was involved was the fact that you always had to give the same information over and over again to different officials in different organisations, or even on different floors of the same organisation. What if that singular inefficiency, that entanglement, was our only hope? What if bureaucracies were efficient?

CONCLUSION
The Unravelling

Admission into the civil service is indeed generally sought after, but it is for the unambitious and the indolent or incapable that it is chiefly desired.

Northcote–Trevelyan Report into the Civil Service, 1853

In 1848, HM Treasury set up an enquiry into the workings of what was then a civil service composed of around 16,000 men, most of whom seem to have been appointed either on nepotistic grounds or for reasons of political pragmatism. In 1853, Stafford Northcote and Charles Trevelyan presented their findings to parliament and, in a single stroke, more or less invented the modern civil service. What they found was a corrupt and self-serving system where the line between politics and paperwork, between The Administration and administration, was utterly blurred and gave rise to potential conflicts of interest of the kind that inspired a dim view of the bureaucrats of the day. Their findings, published as the Northcote–Trevelyan Report, aimed to change all that. They recommended an examination system, a distinction between intellectual and mechanical labour and annual pay increases that were conditional on satisfactory conduct for all staff.

The civil service as we know it today, over 150 years later, is still based on these founding principles. While significant structural change has occurred throughout its history, and the proximity of political power to the institutions of Whitehall represents an ever-present threat to proper conduct and propriety, no subsequent enquiry into the service has found a significant change to the guiding values of impartiality, independence and professionalism. So, why is it that a bad day at the hands of some official or another tempts us to take a similar view to the opening sentiments of Northcote and

Trevelyan – namely, that admission into the civil service is for the unambitious, the indolent or incapable? As the examples in this book show, an exaggerated stereotype lives on, but not without reason.

For instance, we've seen how public bureaucracy has spilled over into the private sector. Middle management's grip on business and commerce has tightened and steadily expanded through meta-work initiatives – such as quality management auditing, quasi-academic review processes, committees, meetings and customer service paradigms apparently borne from one of Kafka's parables. Aided by the interventions of quack consultancies and government alike, the commercial world seems determined to move away from providing products and services and increasingly towards a world of simply talking about it.

In turn, while some would welcome the appropriation of business and management techniques into government and public life, it seems that, along with PR, spin and the other arts of dishonesty, most of the practices that have passed back to the public sector are the new grey orthodoxies of modern middle management – in effect, the same ones begat by the public bureaucracy in the first place. The world of bureaucracy has transformed itself into an Ouroboros, a kind of infinite snake, consuming its own tail – a symbol used throughout history to represent rebirth and infinity. While Margaret Thatcher was railing against government bureaucracy in the early 1980s, private sector red tape was gaining strength. If further proof of the Ouroboros' suitability as an emblem for bureaucracy were needed, Plato described something like an ouroboros as the first living thing in the universe – it 'had no need of eyes when there was nothing remaining outside him to be seen; nor of ears when there was nothing to be heard'. If that doesn't sound like a compelling explanation for your average exchange with Her Majesty's Revenue and Customs, I'm not sure what does.

Causing offence

In Chapter 2, we discovered that there have been a number of surreal new offences created in the last decade, regulating a wide range of minority hobbies from the sale of grey squirrels to the creation of nuclear explosions, but if you thought the few examples of fringe legislation on offer were just that, a fringe, think again. There are many, many new laws: on average, one criminal offence a day – well over 3,000 in total – has been created over the last ten years. For instance, under the Clean Neighbourhoods and Environment Act 2005, if you fail to nominate a neighbour to turn off your burglar alarm while you are on holiday, you are breaking the law. More seriously, it is an offence to spontaneously demonstrate within the designated area up to one kilometre from Parliament Square in London.

Analysis of the new offences reveals that some were updated versions of old crimes and others were temporary – for example, some were regulations passed in order to contain the spread of foot and mouth disease, but even allowing for these exceptions, there has still been an impressive ballooning of regulations available for prosecution. But 3,000 new offences is only scratching the surface, if a study by legal publisher Sweet and Maxwell is to be believed. Len Sealy, the Cambridge University professor of law who carried out the study on behalf of Sweet and Maxwell, estimates that nearly 30,000 laws – one every three hours – have been introduced in the last decade.

With more and more offences come more and more arrests, prosecutions, sentencing and confinement. But even here there are further layers of complexity. Recent figures indicate that even people arrested for trivial offences like littering are routinely having swabs of DNA taken whether they are charged or not. One report even suggests a swab is taken by the police every 45 seconds and that the DNA of up to 150,000 innocent people is held by police forces across the country.

The growing frenzy of legislation has dire implications for us as a state. Quite apart from the civil liberties implications, which are huge, it shows the extent to which a mindset of control and containment has grown within the institutions that govern us. Many of the new laws – particularly, as we have seen, in the field of licensing – give councils new powers of enforcement and increase the potential for on the spot fines or traffic-style fixed penalty notices. Bureaucracies seem to be in the business of acquiring more power.

Yet, all of these larger issues are still dwarfed by the overwhelming sense that life is becoming more about ticking boxes, adhering to inflexible rules and living each day in some kind of Kafkaesque nightmare. Now, wherever we come in contact with the machinery of state, there is the potential for our interaction to turn into a scene from a theatre of the absurd.

Take the new passport photo regulations, for example. What piece of red tape better sums up the state's attitude to us as human beings than the ban on wearing a smile? Enforced for technical reasons – smiles and other facial expressions which reveal the inner character of human beings apparently confuse computers or, rather, they confuse facial recognition systems – it is a typical dehumanising touch. Once more, the needs and quirks of the human become subservient to the needs and quirks of a system. Did you ever feel more like a cog in a machine, relentlessly complying with the requirements of an inflexible process?

The process involves fewer and fewer people and more and more automation, with an attendant concentration on the digital, yes/no, machine-readable tick-box answer to a problem – in that way, the bureaucracy is becoming more and more like a young child, in that it can only see the world in black and white. Most lives are a messy grey. Theoretically, that becomes even more important in the private sector, where the profit motive means that the outcomes of decisions are either profit or loss, meaning that decision-making itself has to be rigidly calculable. In his writing on bureaucracy, the German economist Max Weber identified that the 'more completely it succeeds in achieving the exclusion of love, hatred and every purely personal, especially irrational and incalculable, feeling from the execution of official tasks', the more appropriate it becomes for capitalism.

Weber believed, in the opening years of the 20th century, that further bureaucracy was inevitable. 'Imagine the consequences of that comprehensive bureaucratisation and rationalisation which already today we see approaching. Already now … in all economic enterprises run on modern lines, rational calculation is manifest at every stage. By it, the performance of each individual worker is mathematically measured, each man becomes a little cog in the machine and, aware of this, his one preoccupation is whether he can become a bigger cog.'

These were rare notes of caution from a man who believed that bureaucracy was the mark of a modern and superior society. He compared it, in a modernist way, to the superiority of machine production to handcrafted goods. Today, we crave the handmade, the personal, the things shaped by humans, over and above the efficient and practical die-cast output of sterile factories. Similarly, we want the human touch in our dealings with government, institutions and business – we want to talk as directly as possible to someone who is in a position to listen and to act.

As it is, we are always left feeling as though we have lost, that we have been palmed off in some way. Along with developments in the political process, bureaucracy serves to keep us away from the people who govern us, but you can come away with exactly the same impression after attempting to deal with a commercial corporation on the phone. It's probably because of the top-down model of management beloved of governments and government-sized companies – information drips down, but it isn't designed to drip up. It's a valve, a one-way process, and getting something done by starting at the bottom and talking your way up the chain of command is as rare an event as the depercolation of coffee.

You often hear politicians' promises to slash red tape and I don't think it is too cynical to suggest that you hear it so often because politicians of all shades know that it is precisely what you want to hear. But you have to admit that having all those layers of complexity between you and power is very convenient for the powerful.

The red tape that used to bind related paperwork together has now become an instrument of control. In politics, it has moved its focus from administrative proprieties to the maintenance of itself – a hierarchical system perfectly, if accidentally, designed to keep people remote from the decisions made about them. In commerce, more money is chiselled out of customers because of the enormous reserves of stamina required to engage with a large company in the first place, never mind making a complaint, getting a refund or finding someone who takes you seriously. It's no wonder that call centre staff complain of customers being rude to them; by the time you've negotiated the Byzantine menu system you will be ready to lash out at something – anything – that represents the company, just one more nice little dehumanising touch borne out of an inflexible system.

It is too easy to characterise modern red tape as a cordon, a 'do not cross' line around government and power, but the truth is more frustrating than that. Unnecessary in this electronic document age to tie papers together, red tape has been largely replaced by its digital version, vast relational databases with extensive, though specialised, snapshots of our information on them. Once the National Identity Register goes live, however, the amount of information held about us centrally will balloon exponentially in size. With this super-database used to prove our identity in the public sector and the commercial world (one of the dubious promises of the scheme), simple mistakes can have far-reaching effects. Instead of just having your tax code stuffed up, your benefits withdrawn or your credit rating hit by a simple bureaucratic cock up, imagine a mistake being made in the fundamental area of your life – that you are who you say you are. You couldn't have a bank account, draw benefits, have a doctor or go to college; your non-status would spread like a virus through the system. Your life would be in ruins for months or even years, if the svelte and streamlined processes we have witnessed in this book are anything to go by. The red tape to worry about is not the sort that ties things up, it is the red tape that connects things together. Unravel that and you really have a problem.

ACKNOWLEDGEMENTS

A book of this kind just can't be written without people dredging through their personal lives and recalling incidents and situations most of us would find deeply irritating. To then ask them to write it all down, potentially reliving horrors and frustrations they would rather forget, is a lot to ask and I'm indebted to all of them for doing such a great job.

Thanks also to my editors Ian Preece and Clare Wallis for gently guiding me and my manuscript through the many stages to print and to my friend and agent Simon Benham for getting the business done. I would also like to extend my thanks to Gwyn Vaughan Roberts, who understood the spirit of the book immediately and supplied the fantastic illustrations at the start of each chapter.

Thanks are also due to Dan Kieran and Prasanth Visweswaran – partners on another project who showed incredible patience while I tinkered with the closing stages of this book while I should have, like them, been tinkering with a 1958 milk float in advance of our epic journey in it across England for a forthcoming book, *Three Men in a Float*.

Finally, thanks to my wife, Kate, who continues to put up with this kind of thing all the time.